Facing the Challenges of Life

DR. IRVIN LLOYD FRANCIS

authorHOUSE®

AuthorHouse™ LLC
1663 Liberty Drive
Bloomington, IN 47403
www.authorhouse.com
Phone: 1-800-839-8640

KJV
Scripture quotations marked KJV are from the Holy Bible, King James Version (Authorized Version). First published in 1611. Quoted from the KJV Classic Reference Bible, Copyright © 1983 by The Zondervan Corporation.

Published by AuthorHouse   08/06/2014

ISBN: 978-1-4969-3240-2 (sc)
ISBN: 978-1-4969-3239-6 (e)

DEDICATED

To my wife, Beryl Victoria Francis, A.A., who was instrumental in inspiring me to give this vivid description of the challenges I encountered, and my son Dwight George Francis M.S., who proofread and retyped the entire autobiography on my behalf.

INTRODUCTION

"Facing The Challenges of Life entails the challenges
encountered by a man born in the countryside of Jamaica who
was brought up by his grandparents. He lost his grandfather
at the age of fourteen. His grandmother had no income and
so he worked to support his grandmother, and himself, while
studying for the third Jamaican Local Examination.
After the death of his grandmother, he migrated to the U.S.A.
with his family where he faced many challenges, which he
overcame, and continued to pursue his studies. He attended
college and university and obtained his A.A. B.S. and P.H.D.
After returning from the Department of Health he returned to
his homeland where he embarked on writing this autobiography.
He had written several songs while in the U.S.A. which
have been copyrighted but have not been published yet.

CONTENTS

Life offers a challenge to each of us and the way that we accept this challenge will greatly influence all our future events. Meeting the challenges of life and triumphing over them gives a satisfying and fulfilling experience.

Chapter 1
FACING THE
CHALLENGES OF LIFE

From the moment one arrives in the world there is a set path laid out for that individual to follow. The path might have great obstacles in the way, but one will have to strive to overcome these obstacles in order to proceed on the path.

My emergence on the path of life was on a Monday afternoon in the month of January at about dusk. It was in the parish of St. Ann, in a little district called Fort George. I grew up at my grandparents home and was informed that my mother had to leave me with them at an early age to seek employment. She would visit me on the weekends whenever it was possible at her parent's home. I could recall that she was a very strict disciplinarian and many times I felt happier when she did not make the visits on a weekend. I grew up without any other brother or sister and was taken to Fort George Primary School by my grandfather Thomas Benjamin and he registered me as Hervin Lloyd Benjamin.

My grandfather was a farmer. He cultivated yams; bananas, sugar cane and he had pimento and coffee on his farm. He also reared pigs and goats and also had a cow. My grandmother took care of the home-washing, cooking, ironing, baking, etc. She was an excellent cook. Her name was Harriet Rebecca Benjamin. My grandparents were Christian folks. My grandfather was a staunch Baptist who walked about three miles to church on Sundays. When my grandmother could not make the journey, she visited the Methodist church, which was just a mile and a half away. I was brought up in the Methodist church and later on I became a member of the choir.

My earlier days at school were exciting. We sang and prayed in the morning, and prayed in the evening before dismissal. I was not living far from school, so I went home for lunch in the days. My grandmother could tell when it was twelve o' clock by observing where the shadow of the building fell at a particular point at that time of day. During the midsummer holidays we were engaged in the reaping of the pimento crops. My grandfather would climb the pimento trees and broke off the branches with the pimento with his hands. He would engage a crook to bring to his reach the far-reaching branches of the pimento.

The pimento were picked and put on a barbeque for drying by sunlight. During the process of drying, the pimento had to be turned frequently so that there was uniform drying throughout. After the drying process the pimento had to be cleansed of all dried leaves, and sticks, and ripe grains which were soft. The pimentos was then put in crocus bags and taken to the merchants for sale.

I excelled in most of my subjects at school with the exception of Mathematics; in math I was only about average. However, I was an exceptional student in reading, even in my junior classes. When I aspired to the upper division, (as it was called in those days) my teacher requested that I take the class in reading lessons most of the time.

The average time in school back then was eight years. At the end of the school years the progressive students would proceed to the study of the Jamaica Local Examinations. There was no graduation after the completion of the school years. When the years of school were all accomplished, the Head master would simply inform you that your school years were over. If you were a brilliant student, you would be given an extra year as a monitor in which you would remain in school and help to assist with the schoolwork in some ways.

The Jamaica Local Examinations consisted of three stages, i.e. First, Second and Third Examinations. Each exam had about eight subjects. If you failed a subject in any of the examinations, you would be required to repeat the entire exam until you were successful in all the subjects. The Third Jamaica Local Examination was the most difficult, and on successful completion of this exam, you were eligible for a job in either a Government Department, or some other private enterprise. The successful completion of the Third Jamaica Local Examination was also a requirement for entering college.

Chapter 2
THE DEATH OF MY GRANDFATHER

It was during a rainy afternoon on the sixth of May 1954 that I received the sad news that my grandfather had expired. I was taking a Science test at school when the teacher called me and said, "I have received news that your grandfather has kicked the bucket". He told me to discontinue the exam and sent me home. My grandfather had been ill for some time and I had hoped that he would recover from his illness, but unfortunately he didn't.

The doctor had been to see him once and gave him medicine, but this was of no avail. On my arrival home, my grandmother was crying and there were a few friends there as well. I have lived with my grandparents for about fourteen years now and I wondered how things would be without my grandfather around. One of my aunts visited frequently when my grandfather was ill, but her visits were only for short intervals, and I was the only one there permanently with my grandmother. I thought about the reaping of the pimento crop during the midsummer holidays and the role played by my grandfather in harvesting the crops.

I thought about the cultivating of yams and the many other responsibilities that my grandfather assumed; in addition to that, I could not express how much I missed my grandfather. I loved him dearly. When I could accompany him to the distant field around the time that I was about three or four years old, I would aim for his footsteps and tried to put my footsteps exactly where he stepped. He was my father figure. He was very hard working. He was prayerful and an outstanding gentleman in the community. I never looked at my grandfather when he died. I just wanted to remember him the way he was. During the period when my grandfather passed away, preparations were made locally and the burial took place as early as the preparations were completed. The casket was made by the carpenters in the area, who came and assisted with the funeral, and the grave was dug by the gravediggers in the area. There was no funeral parlor and the local residents did everything.

The funeral procession took place at the home and was officiated by the Minister. There were lots of mourners who were greatly saddened by the departure of my grandfather. They expressed how much good he had done for the people in the community and how much he would be missed. Finally my grandfather was laid to rest in the family plot. After the passing of my grandfather it was very lonely around the house. There was a lady and her child who slept at our home until the ninth night was past. One of my aunts also accompanied us a few nights, but when they did not turn up because of rain, or other circumstances it was my grandmother and I alone. One night I dreamt that my grandfather came in the home and looked on my grandmother and I, and said "In peace lay down and sleep, in peace"; when I awoke I was a bit frightened and trembled for a little while.

I had to assume tremendous responsibility for the home and still continued my studies for the local examinations. My grandmother had no income and there was no Government assistance for the elderly folks back then.

There was a gentleman who bought some trees from my grandmother, which he used to produce coal that was sold to some of the residents around the adjoining districts. Later on I acquired the skills of producing coal for our own use in addition to supplementing our finances. Producing coal is one of the most difficult tasks to be performed. The trees were hewed down by axe and cut into pieces about three feet long. A small area of ground was carved out depending on the amount of wood intended to be used. The wood was then laid down on the ground allowing a space in the center for a fire, which was fueled by dried wood.

The rest of the heavier wood was then placed on the top of the lighter wood after the flame ignited. After this the wood was covered with grass, and earth was gradually placed on top of the grass to prevent the flame from consuming the grass that was placed on top of the wood. After all the wood has been covered thoroughly so that only steam seemed to be coming from the coal kiln, it was then left to burn for a few days. It was observed at intervals to make sure that the fire was contained inside and did not break out. The coal kiln was tested by inserting a piece of metal inside to see if the wood had been converted to coal. The coals were then pulled from the kiln and covered with earth to put out any existing flame on the coals. The coals were then packed in bags and ready for delivery to customers.

Transportation was also a great problem in the country. In order to reach Kingston one had to get the "Star bus" which passed at 4:00 am. There was another bus, which traveled in the evening, which was the "Magnet bus". This bus was only suitable for market folks and others travelling to see their relatives in Kingston. Since the bus reached Kingston in the night it could not be utilized by folks who had to go to Kingston and returned the same day.

On one occasion on travelling to Kingston I went to get the bus too early. Our clock was in a state of disrepairs, and so after taking an early nap, I misjudged the time completely. Later on I figured that I went to the bus stop at about 11:00 pm. I spent hours waiting for the bus that night.

On another occasion I overslept. When I awoke I realized that I had to hurry for the bus would be on its way. The distance to the bus stop was over a mile. As I started out I could hear the horn of the bus in the distance away. I raced through a shortcut but I missed the bus by a few seconds. I yelled and yelled, hoping that someone in the bus would see me but they didn't. As a result of that I had to travel about five miles to Kellits to get the McCauly's bus. Such was life in the country those days. These things however never deterred me from focusing on my goals. I worked my way through the Local Examinations. I had to repeat a few before I was successful, but I was determined to achieve this goal.

Finally, I was successful in the Third Jamaica Local Examination, and I was offered a job at the Fort George Primary School as a probationary teacher. I was paid twelve pounds per month, and I was able to purchase better clothing and articles of food for my grandmother and myself. Our home was located on a lonely spot in the village and I never stayed out late knowing that my grandmother would be home alone. After passing the Third Local Jamaica Exam, I had to give up some of the duties that I was engaged in before.

I was now able to employ some of the lads to assist with the fieldwork and clearing some of the thickets around.

During my tenure at the Fort George School, one of my aunts that lived elsewhere returned to stay with my grandmother and I. My grandmother divided the property among the children, and I was offered a portion of the property for sale, which included her share.

I bought that portion of the property but left it for my grandmother to reap all the crops and make use of anything on the property.

Chapter 3
ENTRY INTO THE JAMAICA SCHOOL OF AGRICULTURE

By then, I had applied for entry to the Jamaica School of Agriculture (J.S.A). My mother, who had assisted me with tuition at the Fort George Primary School, wanted me to go to Mico Training College but I loved gardening and preferred to enter J.S.A. I took the interview for the Jamaica School of Agriculture but weeks passed and I did not hear from them. Finally I got a letter that I was accepted. There was a long list of clothing and other items, which I should take with me. The period of time for me to acquire those things was short. I was not given adequate notice. However, despite that, I decided to enter the J.S.A.

My aunt had now moved back to stay with her mother just before my entering into the agricultural school. Her other sister was married and was not living far away. My grandmother would visit her sometimes but she never stayed overnight.

I entered school feeling a relief that my grandmother would not be alone. Shortly after entering the school, I contracted pneumonia and became very ill. There was a lot of hazing by the minority group but what effected me mostly was to be awakened about midnight to take what was called the 'Farmer's Bath.'

About four of us were in each dormitory. There was no air conditioning. It was very hot and I became ill after taking the bath. I was removed to a place they call the Sick Bay. The nurse gave me

Panadol and Corecidin B. I could only drink orange juice for a while. The coughing was terrible; I even coughed up blood. When I recovered and went back to class, I was far behind in my studies. We had to wake up about 5:30 A.M. to go to the farm. We would get a cup of cocoa and a few crackers. When we returned from the farm, there were just a few minutes to take a bath and hurry to get breakfast before rushing off to class.

The subjects were new to me. Chemistry, physics, and much more advanced math. I realized that most of the students had prior learning in these subjects. They had either attended Knockalva, Homewood, or Denthil training centers. I was just a Third Jamaica Local Exam student with no prior training, plus the time that I was ill with pneumonia made it impossible for me to compete. In addition, there was an instructor who was always picking on me. There was no class that he did not have to call on me to answer questions. I resented him, as he was not making my life any easier.

One of the other elements I was missing at the Jamaica School of Agriculture was insufficient suits. I had many pants and shirts but only one suit. We were required to wear suits to supper and it was humiliating to be wearing the same coat on all occasions. My aunt that was married gave me one of her husband's coats, which I wore once to supper, and I was swallowed up by the coat. One of the minorities made some unfavorable remarks about the coat and I never wore it again.

After completing my first term I returned home for the holidays. My grandmother and my aunt that was staying with her were now living at my other auntie's home due to a fire, which devastated their home. Her husband was a farmer and she operated a grocery store. I was engaged in various activities during the holidays such as helping in the grocery store, milking cows, and attending to the animals at the home. There was no time to study; I was constantly engaged in one activity or another.

After the holidays I returned to school and tried to catch up on a few subjects that I had some low grades in, but I was still behind in my studies.

The final term came for our exams and I joined a few study groups. I observed that my method of studying from the primary school had to be changed. During my local exam, we were given notes by the teacher on each subject and he would call on us individually to recite these notes as a recitation. We did not have many of the books to study the subject matter in detail. At Jamaica School of Agriculture there was a set of textbooks to read after the lectures. Nobody could think about studying lessons and reciting them. After we completed the final examinations we went home and awaited the results. When the result arrived, I learned that I had failed two subjects. I was 1.5 percent below the passing grade. I could have asked to repeat the course but decided not to go back to J.S.A. That one-year was enough for me.

Chapter 4
ACTING AS PUBLIC HEALTH INSPECTOR IN ST. ANN

After failure at J.S.A., I made an application to the Health Department in St. Ann. I waited patiently for the reply and finally there was a letter from the Chief Public Health Inspector stating that there was no vacancy at present but my application would be placed on file and I would be contacted if necessary. After a few weeks I wrote another letter and finally I was visited by the Chief Public Health Inspector and scheduled for an interview at the St. Ann Health Department on a certain date.

I was interviewed by the Chief Public Inspector, the Medical Officer of Health (M.O.H.), and a Senior Public Health Inspector.

I was successful in my interview and was sent to the Claremont area for two weeks orientation with Public Health Inspector Barrant. After orientation was completed I was assigned a job as the acting Public Health Inspector in the Bensonton area.

During this period of time, general sanitation was very low in the area. There were Insufficient Sanitary Conveniences at many homes. Public Health Inspectors were required to visit 25 homes daily. The terrain was very rough and the job entailed a lot of traveling. I knew the area well and exceeded the target of 400 homes monthly despite my lack of transport by car; all the journeys were done on foot. There were not even any taxis in the area to alleviate the traveling on foot.

After working for about a year I bought a horse and my aunt's husband lent me a saddle. At first, I was very awkward in the saddle. I used to ride donkeys and mules bareback, which were entirely different from riding in a saddle. Gradually I got adjusted to the saddle riding and I was being hailed as an expert rider.

My horse was an excellent galloper. I fed her with corn and grazed her in the best grasslands. After continuing my Public Health job for a while, I purchased a little room for my grandmother for nine pounds, one shilling, and eight pence. Things did not seem to be going very well at my aunt's house with three additional persons living there.

It was a great relief for my aunt and grandmother to move into their own apartment. I built a Sanitary Convenience and kitchen for them, and had the land surveyed and registered.

After accomplishing this task I started to gather materials for building my own home. During the construction of my home I was recommended to apply for entry to the West Indies School of Public Health. I had worked very hard and improved the standard of sanitation in the area from 45 percent to 85 percent. The Chief and Senior Public Health Inspector held me in high esteem. I missed my first interview for the W.I.S.P.H. due to my involvement in building my home.

I was paid a visit by the Chief P.H.I. who reiterated the importance of training at the West Indies School of Public Health. I was recommended for the next interview at the W.I.S.P.H. By this time my home was almost finished with the exception of the windows.

On the day of the interview, I was questioned by many tutors from the W.I.S.P.H. I answered the questions satisfactorily, both on the written and oral examination

Chapter 5
ADMISSION TO THE WEST INDIES SCHOOL OF PUBLIC HEALTH

The Health Department informed me at a later date that I was selected to enter the W.I.S.P.H for a training of ten and a half months. This training was the equivalency of two years in the U.K. At the end of the training, if we successfully completed the course we would be awarded the Local Public Health Certificate, but our work would be sent to London for further examination, and we would be awarded the Royal Society of Health Diploma if we satisfied the Board of Examinations there.

The course paid a stipend of twenty-two pounds, one shilling, and eight pence per month, and from that stipend we had to pay boarding, bus fare, and lunch.

My aunt's husband got me a place to board in Kingston for fourteen pounds per month. I walked to the bus stop in the mornings and took a bus, which took me to the school at 21 Slipe Pen Road.

The course at West Indies School of Public Health was very interesting and the workload was very heavy. We studied Sanitary Science and Technology. We had to visit the abattoir twice weekly for Practical Meat Inspection. We had many lecturers from U.W.I (University of West Indies) in addition to our regular instructors. They were very knowledgeable and were fun to learn from.

There were a lot of subjects to cover and the time was short. On Saturday mornings we attended St. George's College for physics and chemistry. I had some background on these subjects from J.S.A. I did not ask a lot of questions in class but I was a good listener. I was making good grades on all subjects although my standard of education was much lower than my counterparts. I stayed in the top echelon of the class. When we made presentations I was lauded by my colleagues.

During my training at the West Indies School of Public Health, I would send a small portion of my stipend for my grandmother and visited her whenever possible. Near the competition of my courses, my grandmother became ill. When I visited her she was elated to see me and asked me to get water coconuts for her. I went to the farm that I bought and picked a few water coconuts for her. She drank about half of one and I left the rest so that she could have them later on. I could see that my grandmother was very weak. I loved her dearly and I regretted that I was not able to spend more time with her now, but after the weekend I had to return to school. We talked briefly and then I had to say goodbye. It is regrettable that this Sunday afternoon was the last time I saw my grandmother alive.

Chapter 6
THE DEATH OF MY GRANDMOTHER

When I returned to my boarding home I could not sleep during the night. It was just like a coffin was within the room with me. I turned on the light and opened at random a little book that I had entitled "The Imitation of Christ." The chapter that presented itself was entitled "Of the Mediation of Death." I read the chapter and was very disturbed. It spoke about death and the preparation we should make for the afterlife. I closed the book and went back to bed but I still could not sleep. I attended classes on the Monday and kept thinking about my grandmother.

On the Tuesday evening when I returned home from school there was a telegram waiting. I opened it hurriedly and there was the sad news that my grandmother had passed away. I informed the lady that I was boarded with of the sad circumstance and packed my bag to go home. There was a bus strike during the time and I had to take other transportation to get to my destination. I had to stop by the school of Public Health and informed my instructor that I had to leave for the country due to my grandmother's death.

I then proceeded to Kingston and from there I hired a transport. I had to wait for a few hours before I got a car to take me home. When I finally reached home it was 11:30 P.M. My aunt Florence, the married one, told me that my grandmother was laid to rest earlier on that afternoon. She informed me that her mother passed away 1:30 A.M. the Tuesday morning. She further informed me that owing to the fact that she was keeping a little grocery shop in the district where my grandmother was living... she had removed my grandmother to my unfinished home and that was where she died.

I traveled in the night to my house and that is where my other aunt Eflin was asleep. I awoke her and enquired about the funeral procession and we spent most of the rest of the night talking about all that transpired during the funeral procession. The lack of communication in the area prevented one from getting the necessary information on time.

I was devastated that after taking that long journey home I missed my dear grandmother's funeral. I expressed my sad regret that I was not there to pay the last respects to my late grandmother.

Early in the morning, I went to the family plot where my grandmother was laid to rest beside her husband. I spent some time expressing my regret for not being there for her final departure. I knew that she could not hear me, but that was my way of saying goodbye. I was a man who cried inside and deeply mourned the loss of my grandmother. I tried to comfort myself by reminiscing on the good times we had together singing hymns, praying, going to the market, going to church, and the many words of wisdom that she taught me. I recalled how I would look out for her when I did not accompany her to the market, and due to the fact that our home was located at a very high elevation, I could spot her from miles away and would race down the hill to meet her and carry her basket home. I remembered the good meals we had together. I recalled our struggle together after the death of my grandfather, and how I endeavored to take care of her. These are the memories I'll forever keep.

Chapter 7

FINAL TERM AT WEST INDIES SCHOOL OF PUBLIC HEALTH

The following day I returned to classes and continued my studies for my final term. There were a lot of lectures to cover. Sometimes during our lunch hour we were amazed to see the amount of written material, which was placed, on our desks.

The lessons were very informative however, and there was no turning back. I was asked to write something for the yearbook and I wrote about cleanliness and hygiene, and my classmates liked it.

They also featured me in the yearbook with the following quote- "*Soft spoken and quiet yet well informed, always ranks among the best in the form.*"

Finally our ten and a half months of study was completed with a final examination lasting for several days. The examination was divided into two parts, an oral and a written examination. After the exam there was a state of unrest among us until the results were posted. We were all successful in the finals. I was ranked in the top ten as usual.

We then prepared for Graduation. Graduation day was one of the most exciting days of my life. The Valedictory address was given by our top man of the class- Joel Dhue. He spoke eloquently and emphasized the knowledge imparted to us by the instructors, and the depth of their wisdom. We were elated in receiving our local certificates and the joy of now being qualified as a Public Health Inspector.

After graduation I was still assigned to the Bensonton area. I made recommendations for a grant to build sanitary conveniences for Indigent Parties in a few of the districts and this was approved. Shortly after completing my home I was given a transfer to the Discovery Bay area, but I asked if the transfer could be waived for a while. My request was granted for a short time.

I then got married to a beautiful lady from that area. Our wedding ceremony was lovely. We had guests from many different areas. My wife had many relatives in the area and many that came from abroad. A reception was held at the bride's home and one at my aunt's home. Everything was delightful and we had a fair day. The minister who officiated at the marriage ceremony was very young and said we were his first married couple.

Chapter 8
TRANSFERRED TO WORK IN THE CAPITAL OF THE PARISH

A couple of months after my marriage my transfer came up again for the St. Ann's Bay area. I accepted the transfer. They stated that they wanted a trained Inspector working in the urbanized area where more expertise and knowledge was required. I boarded in the area for a while and then decided to travel daily.

This was extremely difficult owing to the fact that I did not possess a car at the time. Transportation was infrequent. I arose early each morning and got home mostly at night. Fridays were the most taxing days because this was Meat Inspection Day. I had a market in my area and many butchers came in late. I had to wait to have their meat inspected. By the time this was over, the few available transports were gone and the waiting could take hours because there was not any definite transportation that you could build your hopes on. I remembered getting home 1:30 A.M. on one of those Friday nights. When once asked by one of my colleagues about the latest time I ever reached home, I told him 1:30 A.M. He jokingly said, "I don't mean the other day, my friend." It was a great laughter between us.

In addition to my regular duties in the St. Ann's Bay area I was assigned the duties of orientating trainees for the job.

Chapter 9
POST GRADUATE STUDIES AT WEST INDIES SCHOOL OF PUBLIC HEALTH

After working in this environment for about two years, I was recommended by the Parish Council with another officer to do the Post Graduate course in Meat and Other Foods. This was a shorter course of about three and a half months but was very comprehensive.

A greater emphasis was placed on food Hygiene and Meat Inspection. We visited the abattoir three days a week. The odor there was obnoxious but after a while it appeared as if we were immune to it. Meat Inspection involved both ante mortem and post mortem examinations. Oxen, sheep, goats, and pigs were being slaughtered. We studied where the lymph nodes were located and had to incise them on inspection to detect if there was any disease. Meat Inspection necessitates very keen eyes. The improper inspection of diseased carcasses could result in illness and even death. We studied meat inspection by Thornton thoroughly.

During this course, field trips were made to dairies, bakeries, food establishments, and slaughterhouses to observe the level of Sanitation that was practiced. These field trips were great educational tools. Our field guide was quite knowledgeable in all the various areas of meat and other food inspection.

At the completion of this course there was a practical and oral examination. Both parts of the examination were difficult and time for preparation was short. However, my friend K.O. and I felt that we had done justice in satisfying the examiners.

After completing the examination, my friend K.O. accompanied me to purchase a car. It was a 1968 Austin Cambridge. My friend drove back the car to the campus after I completed the transaction because I had not yet acquired my driver's license. When we reached back to campus the results were already posted. We were successful in the examination, but there was one failure in our group and that made us sad.

K.O. drove my car to my home in the country and took back the bus to Kingston to pick up his car. Finally it was graduation and we were attired in our best outfit. My wife and my mother attended my graduation and were elated when I received my diploma. We had a ball on our graduation night and enjoyed ourselves until about midnight.

When my friend and I returned to our Parish, we were greatly applauded on our successes and continued to work in our previous areas. My friend was of tremendous support in assisting me with transportation until I received my driver's license.

Shortly afterwards I was assigned to the Lyford abattoir where I was engaged in daily meat inspection. At first mainly oxen were being slaughtered but afterwards, a large number of pigs from the Agricultural Marketing Corporation were daily brought to the abattoir for slaughter. This greatly increased the volume of work and involved longer hours at the abattoir. Sometimes the pigs were brought in during the late evening hours and slaughtered, awaiting meat inspection in the morning.

After working at the abattoir for some time, I was asked if I would accept a temporary transfer to the Parish of St. Thomas to act as a Grade I Inspector for another officer who was on leave. I accepted the offer and drove 106 miles to St. Thomas to take up the position. I boarded in St. Thomas and traveled home on weekends to spend time with my family. The duration of my time spent at St. Thomas was 103 days. I was mainly involved in Meat Inspection and inspection of Food Handling establishments. Health Education was strongly emphasized in improving the level of hygienic standards in both areas.

When I returned to the Garden Parish I continued to work at Lyford abattoir. During this period I became acquainted with two veterinarians Dr. Schloss and Dr. Barnes. These veterinarians were experts in Meat Inspections and it was a pleasure for me to work with them. I seized every opportunity to increase my knowledge of meat inspection with the experts.

The veterinarians, having seen my interest in Meat Inspection, informed me that they would recommend me for a Pan American health Organization (P.A.H.O.) Fellowship to study meat inspection at the United States Department of Agriculture (U.S.D.A.) for about two months. I continued working at the abattoir for a few weeks and then I received news that I was recommended for a P.A.H.O. Fellowship to the U.S.D.A.

Chapter 10
MY FIRST TRIP TO
THE UNITED STATES

Dr. Schloss took care of all the necessary documents for the trip and informed me of the date of departure. When I arrived at the airport, Dr. Schloss was there to brief me on the trip and gave me my itinerary. I also received an amount in U.S. funds to defray my expenses while I was in the United States. There were a few more Public Health Inspectors at the airport that boarded the airline with me for the United States.

Shortly after boarding, Delta Airlines took off to the U.S. This was my first flight on an airplane and the trip was very exciting. After landing at New Orleans I discovered that I had missed my connecting flight to Baton Rouge and had to wait about 3 hours for the next flight to Baton Rouge.

Finally I was boarded on my flight to Baton Rouge. The flight on Southern was not as smooth as my flight on Delta Airlines. We encountered a lot of air turbulence but we reached our destination safely. When I arrived in Baton Rouge I had just missed the bus that would take me to the motel. It was already getting late and it would be a few hours before the other bus arrived so I took a cab to my motel. When I arrived at the motel it was night. There was a restaurant a little distance away. I could see the lights in the distant and traveled the distance to get something to eat, for by this time I was very hungry and exhausted. After purchasing something to eat I returned to the motel and made ready for bed.

I awoke early in the morning and attended Steven's Meat Plant to observe Meat Inspection. The operation there was much different from what took place at the Lyford abattoir. This was a much larger operation and all the meat inspection was done by a veterinarian. Carcasses moved along the line very fast and there were both men and women trimming bruises from the carcasses at various points before they entered the cooler. All the intestines, skins, and heads of carcasses were shipped to a section of the abattoir where they were manufactured for animal feed and manure.

There was a lunch truck that arrived on breakfast and lunchtime so that snacks could be available for purchase.

After completing my three weeks of training at Steven's Meat Plant I had to travel to Texas to complete my other four weeks of training at U.S.D.A. I failed to review my itinerary thoroughly and overlooked that I had a booked flight to Texas so I booked myself on a Greyhound. The bus left about 3:00 P.M. and traveled all night. I reached my destination at dawn and checked into my hotel. A restaurant was located right there which afforded ready access to our meals. At Texas I was re-united with all the other trainees who were dispatched to different locations. Our instructors were also veterinarians who started out by giving us an impromptu test. I scored in the low eighties but seventy was the passing grade. The course at U.S.D.A. was very interesting. We studied about a lot of diseases that were new to us and lighting requirements for various establishments.

We had frequent tests throughout the course and a final exam at the completion of the course. We were all-successful in the final examination and received our U.S.D.A. Training Certificates. After the completion of the course we spent a short time viewing a part of the city and purchasing a few things to take home. The flight home was very smooth. The pilot gave frequent announcements of some of the countries he was approaching and the height that he was flying. We had one stop on our way home in Montego Bay. I discovered that some one that was disembarking at Montego Bay took one piece of my luggage but I retrieved it promptly. The party explained that it was done in an error.

We were at Montego Bay for a while and then we boarded again and within a short time we heard the announcement that we were landing at Norman Manley International Airport.

By the time we cleared customs it was nightfall. It was a relief to be back safely in my homeland. A few of us took a cab to take us back to our final destinations. I lived the farthest distance and all of my friends were home before me. I reached home about 11:00 P.M. and was united with my family. I spent a couple of hours telling my wife of my experience on my trip and all that transpired in the foreign land.

After the weekend, I reported back at the Health Department and submitted a detailed report of my training both at Steven's Meat Plant and U.S.D.A. The staffs were impressed of my accomplishments and congratulated me on my recent success. I resumed work at the Lyford abattoir and considered myself more adept in meat inspection.

During meat inspection on a late afternoon I discovered tuberculosis in the lymph nodes of a carcass. It was discovered to be a homogenous dissemination and the entire carcass was condemned as being unfit and unwholesome for human consumption. This led to the inspection of the entire herd, which was slaughtered and inspected under the supervision of a veterinarian.

Before I went on the overseas training it was discussed that meat inspection would be promoted to a higher level and that I would be overseeing meat inspection throughout the Parish after completing the training. After working for a long time this plan did not materialize and I became frustrated. I was recommended to act as Senior Public Health Inspector for a short time to fill in for an officer who went on leave and I accepted the position. Shortly after completing this assignment I attended a course of training for Senior Public Health Inspectors at Hope Gardens in Kingston. This course lasted only for a few days and covered a number of topics including Ante Mortem Inspections, zoonoses, Leptospirosis, etc.

After completing this training I was getting a bit weary and decided to apply for some vacation leave. I made an enquiry about my vacation leave and discovered that I had accumulated 35 days of vacation leave, which was approved on submission.

Chapter 11
THE VACATION THAT CHANGED MY LIFE

I contacted a friend I had in the United States and he invited me to come and spend some of my vacation with him. I had a multiple visa stamped in my passport so I booked my flight for traveling to the U.S. The day before my travel I had many errands to run and also dropped in at the Health Department to say goodbye to my co-workers for a while. The evening before the flight I drove my 1968 Austin Cambridge to my sister-in-law's home in Spanish Town. The road was wet and slippery but I drove slowly and carefully.

After reaching Spanish Town, I left my car at her house and took a cab to the airport. My flight was at 8:00 P.M. I checked in and boarded at the appointed time on Air Jamaica for the U.S. On arrival there, my friend picked me up at the airport and headed to his home. We talked about Jamaica on the way home and he also informed me about his activities in the States. On arrival at his home I was introduced to his wife and we had supper before retiring to bed. In the morning he left for work at dawn. I was so accustomed to early waking that I was out of bed very early and was enjoying the fresh air outside. How unfamiliar the scenes around me looked; there were no mountains or valleys in the area, no bustling brook, but the busy noise of traffic to and fro

I had breakfast, which was prepared by my friend's wife about 10:00 AM. She worked during the night and was not an early riser. I spent the rest of the day organizing things around the yard. I always liked to keep myself busy.

When my friend returned home from work in the evening he informed me that he could file for me as a brother and promised to take me one of the evenings to an Immigration consultant. At first I declined this offer but after much persuasion later on, I decided to give it a try. On our arrival at the Immigration consultant's office my friend outlined the circumstance to him and we were informed that this could not be done even though we had similar surnames.

Just before exiting the office the Immigration consultant enquired if I had any relatives that were living in the United States. I told him that my mother had been living in New York for some time. He told me if she was a U.S citizen she could file for me to become a permanent resident. I communicated with my mother while I was on the P.A.H.O Fellowship but we never talked about citizenship. I decided to give her a call and she informed me that she had acquired a U.S. citizenship quite a while back.

On receiving that information I relayed it to the Immigration consultant. He informed me that my mother would have to come to Florida and he would file the papers to adjust my status. I invited my mother down and paid her fare to Florida. She told me that she had just come back from a trip to the Holy Land and had a bit of expenditure. Arrangements were made for the flight and I picked her up from the airport with a cab to my friend's home. Shortly after I made an appointment with the Immigration consultant and my papers were filed to adjust my status.

The downside to this was that I was instructed that I could not leave the country during this period because I would interrupt the entire process. My vacation leave would expire and I could not see my family for quite some time.

I wrote a letter to the Health Department asking for an extension of leave but they informed me to resume work on the expiration of my leave. I had to make a tough decision to either give up my job or remain in the U.S.

After carefully evaluating the situation I decided on the latter. This was a bit risky but life is also about taking risks. During this period of waiting I made application for a Social Security number at the Social Security Administration office. My friend was busy leaving for work at dawn and returning home late in the evenings. I had no one to show me around. I decided to walk around the area and look for job advertisements. One day while I was on the job search I saw a sign. 'Tony Roma, a Place for Ribs.' The doors were closed but my curiosity lead me to take a step and knock on the door. A beautiful waitress opened the door and greeted me. I asked her if they needed any help inside. She invited me inside and told me to wait until she checked with the chef.

A few minutes later, a tall black guy came out and introduced himself as Al. He gave me an application form, which I completed and returned to him. Al reviewed it and brought it to the attention of someone else and they had a brief discussion. He was amazed at my qualifications and told me to see him at 4:30 PM the following evening.

Chapter 12
EMPLOYMENT AT TONY ROMA

When I returned the following evening I was employed and started working at "Tony Roma, a Place for Ribs" as a prep cook. My pay was three dollars an hour and my schedule was 4:00 P.M. – 12:00 P.M.

I was engaged in the preparation of Baby Back Ribs, which was placed in the cooler for the cooks to prepare on the grill for customers. A thin membrane was removed from the underside of the ribs by a large fork after they were thawed out in warm water.

I was also trained to use the dishwater in case of emergency when the dishwasher personnel did not show up. Even cooks operated the dishwasher sometimes when they were short staffed. After a few weeks I was trained to work on the line with the cooks. At first I was only cooking fries, which were served with ribs, stakes, or tidbits.

As time progressed however, I was promoted to a cook. My hourly pay had increased to $4.00 an hour and I was working longer hours. Working on the cook's line was very busy. The waitresses were bringing in the tickets and the orders had to be filled quickly. Friday and Saturday evenings were the busiest times of all. Sometimes you could not take a break until the end of your shift. The job was very demanding but I had to hold on to it for the time.

It was during my tenure at Tony Roma that I received a letter from the Immigration and Naturalization Services to attend for an interview in Miami. I was also required to have a medical test done. I completed the requirements and attended the interview. The interviewer asked quite a few questions and completed the necessary papers for my adjustment of status. He informed me that I could not travel to my country during the time that I was awaiting my Green Card because I would interrupt the entire process. During this time that I was awaiting my Green Card, my wife visited and updated me on all that was happening at home and how the kids were longing to see me. She stayed two weeks before returning home. My job at Tony Roma was even now more demanding. I was working from 7:00 P.M. to 4:00 A.M. The problem was that from 11:00 P.M. to 4:00 A.M. I was working by myself on the cook's line. They assumed that it would not be busy then, but it was always very busy. There were the late eaters that were always coming in and I had to keep running all night long.

After things slowed down the entire working area had to be cleaned. I would then close the restaurant and walked home. I had not purchased a car as yet. On a few occasions one of the waitresses that were working late would give me a ride home. At the end of work, one was extremely exhausted. I was getting to dislike my job. My hourly rate had increased to $4.75 per hour but I felt that this job deserved a better pay. I tried to apply for a managerial position but I was told that there was no vacancy at the present time. I was given a trainee and after he completed training I was informed that he was being paid $5.00 per hour while I was still paid $4.75 per hour. Well, I wondered if it was because he was a white guy and I was black. Anyway, I continued working and came to the conclusion that I would have to get out of that place.

My wife came back for a visit in about four months after she left. On the following day after her arrival we went out to the store to do shopping, and when I returned and checked the mail there was an envelope from the Immigration and Naturalization Service's, which contained my Green Card. I had obtained my permanent visa in six months. I was elated and went and filed for my wife the following day. Things had improved at the immigration consultant's office. The office was now equipped to take photographs and she had it done right there. I had to travel five miles back and forth to take my pictures. I started to look for another job in the advertisement section of the Daily gleaner and saw that they were employing cooks at the Hilton Hotel in Inverrary.

I decided that I would check out the Hilton the following day before work. That night after working at Tony Roma and cleaning the work area, I stayed for a while and looked around the place. I heard an inner voice saying, "Goodbye Tony Roma, this is my last night with you." I walked out the restaurant and went home.

The following day I made a call up to the Hilton Hotel and spoke with a lady who told me that I should come in for an interview at 2:00 P.M. the same day. I went for the interview and was employed instantly. My hourly rate was $5.00 per hour and my schedule was 2:00 P.M.-10:00 P.M. I called the chef at Tony Roma and resigned my job there and assumed my new position at the Hilton Inn of Inverrary.

Chapter 13
NEW POSITION AT THE HILTON INN OF INVERRARY

When I assumed duties at the Hilton Inn of Inverrary one of the challenges that I faced was the distance that I would have to travel daily. The distance from home was much further than the distance from Tony Roma. Fortunately I met a gentleman who was the Head cook there who was living not more than about a quarter mile from my home and we worked out a traveling arrangement, which was quite feasible.

My job at the Hilton was mainly preparing fruits, vegetables, and various sandwiches for customers. The gentleman that worked on the morning shift was very experienced in this type of occupation and thus helped to relieve me a bit depending on how busy he was in the A.M. There were days however, when there was nothing left over from the A.M. and I had to do everything from scratch, and this made my day horrible. Sometimes I was assisted by my friend who I worked out the traveling arrangements with when things were slow on the cooking line.

During my employment at the Hilton Inn of Inverrary, I had taken both the State Required Examinations for Sanitarian 1 and the Hotel and Restaurant Inspection. I received information that I was successful in both examinations. I made an application for the Hotel and restaurant Inspection, but I was told that they were not hiring, and that the department was in the process of reorganizing. I then applied to the Broward County Health Department for a position as Sanitarian

1. The advertisement read that a four-year degree was required but those who had experience in the field and not holding four year degrees were eligible. I was interviewed by the Director of Environmental health and did pretty well on the interview. At the end of the interview, he informed me that he would contact me early about the position. I waited for a while and then I decided to pay him a visit and enquire about the position. The Director informed me that of all the applicants that he had interviewed, I was the most experienced but the problem was that I was not yet a citizen of the U.S. and I did not have a degree.

I tried to make my case about the advertisement that read that applicants that had prior Public Health Experience would be eligible for the job. He told me that they had withdrawn that section from the news advertisement.

I left the Health Department disappointed and continued my job at the Hilton Inn of Inverrary. During this period, my wife also received her Green Card and was gainfully employed. Applications were already filed for our children to join us in the States. We had made application for a certified copy of my income Tax Statement from the Internal Revenue Department as required, but this was not yet received. I went to Miami to check on the status of the children and discovered that the office was relocated and the documents for two of our children were lost, and I would have to re-file for them. This was done on the same day with the assistance of the Immigration officer and placed in the mail.

The good news however was that two of our children were approved for entry to the United States. I needed to visit the Embassy in Kingston with my certified Income Tax Reports for final approval. My Income Tax Report was delayed so I decided to take a non-certified copy of the report to Jamaica. On arrival there, they informed me that the certified copy of the report was required. I was accompanied by my wife and we spent a few days with our kids at our relative's house before returning to the U.S.

On arrival home, I received my certified Tax Report and forwarded it to my sister-in-law who submitted it to the Embassy for approval and took up the two children to the U.S. on October 17, 1980. Shortly afterwards the other two children were also approved and were also taken by their aunt to join the rest of the family.

Our family was united again and our children started school in the U.S. On one of the doctor's visits with two of the children, the doctor enquired what type of employment I was engaged in and when I informed him he advised me to enroll in college. He said, "Irvin, I see that you are a very intelligent fellow but this country is funny; if you work nights, go to school in the day, and if you work in the day, go to school at nights." I took his advice and enrolled at the Broward Community College. My wife had started college prior to that. I believed that having passed the States Required Examination I would be eligible for employment with the Health Department but I was greatly disappointed. I took only six credits at BCC the first term in religion and English literature. On the final examination I made A's on both subjects.

I then took twelve credits the next term and ended up with A's and B's. As I advanced in these courses I encountered more difficulty in subjects such as statistics, accounting, and mathematics but I persevered. I made the Dean's List one semester and I finally had my Associate of Arts in Business Administration. Before I completed my course I applied for a job as Sanitarian I with the Dade County Health Department and I was successful in my interview for the position. The job would be paying me $12.00 more biweekly than my present job at the Hilton. I had just purchased a 1982 Toyota Corolla. The job paid no upkeep for your car as in Jamaica, and the traveling from home to the job, which was over 30 miles one way, paid no mileage for that traveling. The Interviewing officer informed me that there was no vacancy near to the Broward County line and they would be appointing me a position in Key West.

When I returned home after evaluating the position correctly, the following day I called up the department and declined the position. I proceeded to take my education a step further having now attained my A.A. Degree. I applied for entry to Florida Atlantic University. The course work was much more advanced and I could only take six credits per semester. I had acquired a new job at Vision ease, which entailed working some machines for downsizing glasses for making lens. The machines were very difficult to set up and had to be on curves. The molds that were made were thoroughly inspected for scratches, broken edges, and also had to be on curves. The schedule was from 4:00 P.M. to 12:15 P.M., but occasionally we were required to work an hour mandatory overtime and sometimes five hours also on Saturdays.

A weekly report of your performance was given on Mondays. The report detailed how many molds were made by each worker and the percentage that was good and the percentage that was bad. A high percentage of 90% and upwards was the required standard for good molds. Performance was measured based on quantity and quality.

Each mold that was manufactured bore your initials for identification. The job kept you on your feet most of the working hours. Each employee operated three machines and close attention had to be paid so that the molds did not downsize too much. The molds had to be measured at intervals until the required measurement was attained. The machines were timed for each mold and each completed batch was taken to an inspector for inspection.

My days were filled with work, traveling to F.A.U. to attend classes, and hurrying home to get to work at 4:00 P.M. Sometimes I was involved in some group exercises and I had to write an article for the paper and my classmates would pick up the article so that it could be embodied in the paper for the group. This caused me to dislike group work because it placed a great stress on me. Many students lived on campus and had all the time to do these things but I had very little time. Most of the studies were done after I returned from work at nights and on weekends.

After accumulating a certain amount of credits at F.A.U., I submitted my credentials to the Regents College for evaluation. I received a report that I needed 15 more advanced credits in the areas of business for the completion of my Bachelor's Degree in Business and I could take these courses from any accredited college. I continued to take credits at F.A.U. and I applied to the University of Nebraska, which offered courses on Independent study. I completed six credits at F.A.U. and nine credits at the University of Nebraska.

After completing my course work at these institutions successfully, I had these credits submitted to the Regents College. The name was now changed to the University of the State of New York. After waiting for a few weeks, I received a report from the University that I was now eligible for graduation. I completed the necessary paper work along with the required fees and submitted them to the University of the State of New York.

Having achieved this measure of success, I made an application to the Health Department for a position as an Environmental Health

Specialist. I was interviewed by the same Director of Environmental Health who interviewed me a few years ago. He was amazed to see me and congratulated me for having completed the requirements for my Bachelor of Science in Business. I had not yet received my diploma but I had my letter and transcript from the university. He did not even look at my documents. I answered all the interviewing questions and was offered the position. I requested to give my employer at Vision Ease two weeks' notice before assuming the position.

The folks at Vision Ease expressed regret that I was leaving and congratulated me for having completed my studies and wished me success in my new position. On the final day a send off party was made for me and I was given a beautiful Seiko watch by my colleagues. Finally, my night shift jobs were coming to a close. I had worked for twelve and a half years on night shifts and attended classes during the days. This was no easy task but I had faced the challenges and conquered the prevailing circumstances.

Chapter 14
EMPLOYMENT AT THE BROWARD COUNTY HEALTH DEPARTMENT

I reported for work at the Broward County Health Department on the 2nd of November 1990 for orientation. There were a few other employees there for orientation also. After completing all the necessary paper work and the necessary briefing I was dispatched to the Davie Area and met the Supervisor who informed me that I would be doing the Inspection of Public Swimming Pools. He also informed me that I should report to another officer at the Hollywood office for two weeks training in Pool Inspection. I spent the rest of the day reading office manuals pertaining to procedures and practices of the Health Department.

I arrived at the Hollywood Health Department the following morning at 7:45 A.M. and met my new officer for orientation. We visited a number of pools and checked the PH and chlorine levels, safety features, and the type of filters in the pool house. My instructor had a clipboard with a Pool Inspection form, which had all the requirements for pool inspection. He just ticked the conditions which was okay and made an 'X' for the conditions that were bad. A few pools were closed temporarily and notices served for the unsatisfactory conditions to be corrected.

I was amazed at the variation between Public Health work in the U.S. and in my country. Pool Inspection, for instance, was just one phase of my inspection on a daily routine, in addition to inspection of bakeries, and hotels, restaurants, food shops, other premises, meat inspection, etc. It was unbelievable that with my Public Health background I was not offered employment in Broward County prior to having four-year college degree. The Public Health Inspector that is trained at the West Indies School of Public Health was trained in all phases of Public Health and qualified to operate as a Public Health Inspector anywhere. On the other hand, the Environmental Health Specialists here knew nothing about Public Health although he or she has a four-year college degree. He or she could major in history, business, or other sciences and the experience in Public Health would be the short training of two weeks on orientation with someone working in that field.

Finally I completed my two weeks orientation and was sent back to work in my assigned area. The job entailed a lot of traveling and at the end of the day a return was made to the office to update the records. There was no upkeep on your car as in my country and the traveling was just 20 cents per mile. The job offered no variety and became monotonous after a while. Shortly after assuming duties at this office location our office was relocated about six miles further north.

I was just traveling about two miles to the office and now I had to travel four miles more. After moving to this office location for about two months, the office was again relocated to about eight miles further north in Pompano. This made it extremely difficult after completing work in the field to return to the office in the evening. You had to report to the office before work in the morning and to report after work in the afternoon. Traveling was only reimbursed from the office to the work location and back. At the end of the day on reaching home, I was exhausted. I thought about the struggle I faced before acquiring this position and how things were much different from what I anticipated.

After continuing in the job for a few more months, news was received that the department was downsizing and only a few officers who had a long work history would be retained. I had only ten and a half months with the Health Department. The Director of Environment Health told me that I had accumulated more points than my newer counterparts but he could not guarantee my retention in the department. We were given notices regarding the termination of our employment.

Well, I realized that I could not await this uncertainty and so I applied for a job as a Health Services Representative in TB Control. I was called for an interview by the Community Health Nursing Supervisor. She was greatly impressed by my knowledge and experience in Public Health. She informed me that I would hear from her in a few days. I had very good appraisals on my job as an Environmental Health Specialist and I was told that if there was an opportunity for the department to retain any of the new employees, it would be me, however, this was not something on which I could rely on, so I took the necessary action. Within three days I received a phone call from the C.H.N.S. stating that I was selected for the job as a Health Services Representative. Only a few weeks had expired from my month's notice of termination and so I informed the Department of my new position and was released after two weeks to take my new position in TB Control.

Chapter 15
NEW POST AS HEALTH SERVICE REPRESENTATIVE

When I took my new position in TB control, my job title was changed to Health Services Representative. There was one other individual with me from Environmental Health whom I had not met before. He was working in another phase of Environmental Health other than Pool Inspection, and was also successful in obtaining a position with TB Control.

We were given brief training by the C.H.N.S. and he was assigned to work in the southern area of the county and orientated by a former Health Services Representative. I was assigned to the northern area of the county. The C.H.N.S. took me to the Sunrise area and the Pompano area and introduced me to the TB monitors at both locations. The TB monitors were registered Public Health Nurses. The C.H.N.S. briefly acquainted me with the duties of the H.S.R. as we made a few field visits.

On one occasion, we visited a client in the Sunrise area who was diagnosed with TB and was placed on medication by the doctor in charge of TB Control. On our visits to the client, it was observed that she was not taking her medications. The bottles that contained the medication were stocked in cupboards in her house and very few of the pills were taken out of a few bottles. Some bottles were left completely unopened. The C.H.N.S. stressed the importance of taking these medications as prescribed in order to be cured of this disease. The client was also informed that I would be taking her to the Sunrise Health Center at 8:30 in the mornings so that she could take her medication under the supervision of one of the Health Nurses there who worked in TB Control.

The following morning I arrived at the client's home at 8:30 A.M. to take her to the Sunrise Health Center. I knocked on the client's door for about ten minutes before she responded. The client came out with her medications and told me that she overslept. I took her to the clinic and she was observed taking her medications, and I took her home afterwards. On the way home, the client coughed a bit but I gave her tissues and instructed her to cover her mouth when coughing to prevent the transmission of the disease. After taking the client to the clinic for a few days, I suggested to the C.H.N.S. at the main office that instead of transporting the client to the clinic daily, I could see the client take her medications in the home. She said this was an excellent idea and that some plans were in motion to make it a reality.

In the days I would be at the Health Center in Sunrise and return to the main office in the evenings. The clinic days at Sunrise were Tuesdays, and Thursdays at the North Regional Health Center. I was reading up on tuberculosis and acquainting myself gradually with my responsibilities as a Health Services Representative (H.S.R.).

On Mondays, I reviewed the medical records of the clients, which had appointments at the Sunrise Health Center on Tuesday, and tried to contact them by phone to remind them of their appointments. The clients that I was unable to contact during the daytime I would call later from my home. On my first clinic day at the Sunrise Health Center the nurses that worked in the clinic were busy all day. There was a huge turnout of clients for their appointments. Many of the nurses were alarmed at the turnout. I overheard nurses discussing that they did not know why they were so busy on that day and it used to be so slow.

During their discussion, an elderly nurse came by and told them that the turnout was due to the efforts of the new Health Services Representative who was busy reminding clients of their appointments. They conceded that she was right.

On Tuesdays I remained in the clinic and spent some time with the doctor in charge of TB Control. I was learning about X-rays and would ask the Director questions on tuberculosis. On Thursday mornings I took X-rays to the Director of TB Control at the North regional Center and spent time in the clinic there too. I would also remind the clients in the North Regional area of their clinic appointments on Thursdays and the turnout of clients for their appointments were also great.

On days that were not clinic days I would go to look for clients that were lost to follow up by the previous Health Services Representative. The names of the clients were made available to me by the TB monitors in both regions. I had difficulty sometimes locating some of the clients in the North Regional area. Some of them had moved and left no forwarding address. More clients had now been placed on medication and my workload was getting heavier. My job was also getting more exciting and I was able to use some of my Public Health expertise in solving many of the problematic situations.

By this time approval was given for clients to take their medication in their homes under the supervision of the Health Services Representative. I would meet with the clients and discuss the designated times for the home visits to observe them taking their medications. The time had to be agreeable for both client and the H.S.R. This procedure was the birth of what was officially termed Directly Observed Therapy (DOT). Under Directly Observed Therapy, on a visit to the client's home the client had to take all the medications at once. The pills from each bottle were checked and the H.S.R. would observe the client swallowed each dosage of the medication. The medications were taken with water or juice. After the client had swallowed each dosage of the medication, the dosages were recorded on a log by the H.S.R. and the client had to sign their name on the log, which also bears the signature of the H.S.R.

During these home visits, the clients were educated on the transmission and prevention of TB. Before a cure was discovered for TB, millions of people died from the disease, which was known as consumption, the white plaque, wasting disease. Thanks to Dr. Robert Koch, who isolated the causative organisms known as Mycobacterium Tuberculosis. With the Advent of modern drugs such as Isoniazid, Rifampin, Ethambutol, Pyrazinamide, etc. the disease was no longer dreaded as the number one killer.

As time progressed, my workload was getting extremely heavy. I was the only Health Services Representative in the area and the growth of clients had reached an exceedingly great magnitude. Some of the cases were extremely interesting and a few were also challenging. The following chapter gives a brief synopsis of the cases involved.

Chapter 16
CASES OF DIRECTLY OBSERVED THERAPY

For purposes of not revealing the identity of the clients I will call the first client "A" and the second client "B". Client "B" was previously admitted to A.G. Holly, but after remaining there for a few months, the client was discharged with instructions to continue Daily Observed Therapy at home. Client "B" was visited by the nurse in charge of the tuberculosis clinic for the area and myself. She was also given all the necessary information about Directly Observed Therapy and that I would be managing her case. She was also placed on Directly Observed Therapy twice weekly. I arranged her schedule also for Mondays and Thursdays and the time given was ten o' clock in the morning. Client "B" was living with her mother and her relatives. Fortunately she had a telephone so that she could be contacted if there was an emergency.

Client "B" was quite cooperative at first and I did not encounter this problem of awaking this client, as was the case of client "A". Client "B" also took her medications quite easily without much persuasion but client "A" needed a lot of persuasion sometimes to swallow those pills.

Client "B" was also taking a lesser amount of pills than client "A" because she had already received a great amount of medications at A.G. Holly and her condition was improved prior to the Directly Observed Therapy. All the clients that were on Directly Observed Therapy had the medications kept at their home. Anytime the supply of medications was getting low I would inform the nurse and get another order of medications. I also reported all side effects the client's were experiencing to the nurse so that the M.D. could be informed about the situation. Sometimes the doctor found it possible to discontinue a certain medication or change the order to a new one.

The clients were given appointments at frequent intervals to attend the health centers and have a medical examination done. During this examination, the client's blood pressure, pulse and weight were checked. Sputum was also collected, blood drawn, and a chest x-ray was taken which was also reviewed by the tuberculosis specialist. After this examination was done, the client would be given another appointment for the clinic.

As client "B" continued therapy for some time and her condition continued to improve the client occasionally began to take off sometimes for a weekend and could not be found sometimes on the date for her Directly Observed Therapy. Whenever the client was missed at the regular time, I would return at a later time the same day to see if the client had returned. On one occasion I missed the client at the 10:00 A.M. appointment and I left a message with the mother of the client that I would be returning at noon. As I drove up and enquired for the client, the client also drove up. This client was mobile and was able to get around frequently. I instructed the client to inform me when she was not going to be present so that we could arrange a different schedule. The schedule frequently changed to Tuesdays and Fridays to facilitate the client and the time was also adjusted sometimes to eight o' clock in the morning instead of ten o' clock.

During this period, Client "A" was having a housing problem and had to move back to her mother's home with her kids. She was complaining about some side effects, which she was having such as nausea and I reported this to the nurse who consulted the M.D. The M.D. discovered that she was resistant to Isoniazid and had this medication discontinued. This client was taking seventeen pills altogether on each visit. It was depressing to see this client take all these tablets but I had to persuade her to take them so that she could get well. Many times the client took the tablets with water. She swallowed them easier when she had some juice to take them. Sometimes I would purchase some juice and take them to the client to allow for easier taking of the medications. Directly Observed Therapy calls for drastic measures. The client had to take all the medications at once on the time of visit. Clients that are compliant take a lesser amount of medications each time because the dosage recommended is a smaller amount of tablets between two to four times daily. In this way a smaller amount of tablets is taken each time with less difficulty. When directly observed, therapy is administered twice weekly on Mondays and Thursdays; there is an interval of three days between Thursdays to Sunday that the client does not take any medication, so the massive doses compensated for this time interval without medications.

One thing is for sure; when a client is ordered Directly Observed Therapy there is no doubt that the medications are taken. Each time we make sure that the correct number of medications are counted from each bottle, and see that the clients swallow the medications. I adopt a procedure to have the tablets taken from each bottle, counted, and placed in a small container so that there can be no error with medications. Once the client has all the medications to be taken, the bottles are placed back at their usual place and the client proceeds to take the medications until each tablet is swallowed.

A separate Directly Observed Therapy log is maintained for each client with the name of the client, and the required amount of medications to be taken in milligrams. This medication order is signed by the M.D. On each Directly Observed Therapy visit the date is entered and the amount of medications taken in milligrams for each medication is recorded and signed by the Health Services Representative. As each sheet is completed a copy is made and the original sheet is placed in the client's record and the copy is given to the Senior Human Services Program Specialist. If the client is missed on three successive visits the record is taken to the nursing supervisor for some type of disposition to be made.

After client "A" continued therapy for about four to five months, she had all her sputum and smears confirmed negative and her chest radiograph showed remarkable improvement. The client requested a clearance for work and was given a letter to that effect by the Pulmonary Specialist. The client then informed me that she would like the scheduled time changed from nine o' clock in the morning to one-thirty in the afternoon. One of the interesting things about Directly Observed Therapy is that the person managing these clients has to be very flexible. You must be able to adjust your schedule from time to time to facilitate the client even if it inconveniences you. An important fact that must always be borne in mind is that the interests of the client comes first and exceeds our own. I rearranged the client's schedule to one-thirty in the afternoon. At this time I was covering two clinics and it was a real rush sometimes to reach the client on time but I did.

After this schedule continued for a few weeks, I started to miss the client a few times on the 1:30 P.M. schedule and I had to return later, but sometimes I still did not see the client on the later visit either. Anyway, whenever I missed the client on the appointed day I would return the following day and surprise the client sometimes with an early morning visit. The client complained how difficult it was to take the tablets in the early mornings and she preferred the evening schedule. I advised her to stick to the 1:30 appointment that she had chosen.

Eventually the client asked that the schedule be changed to 3:00 P.M. because after a job search she took the bus and there was considerable delay in reaching home. The schedule was changed to 3:00 P.M. as requested. This schedule was also good for me because it afforded me to visit the other health center and perform the required tasks and get back to this appointment on time. The client told me that she was unsuccessful in her attempts to find a job and that she intended to go to Georgia for a weekend to visit a friend and that she would take her medications with her. I reported this to my supervisor who told me to emphasize the importance of taking the medications to the client although at this phase she was no longer infectious. The client departed for Georgia. I made sure that she had more than enough medications to last much longer than the time she intended to stay. The client stayed in Georgia ten days longer than the time she told us that she would be staying. Several home visits were made but her mother informed me that the client was still in Georgia.

Finally the client returned. She had enough medications to last her up to that duration of time, and she assured me that she took the medications. She gave several reasons for prolonging her stay and expressed how much she was sorry. By this time another M.D. visit was due for the client. The client had now completed six months of therapy and her weight had improved to 155 pounds. Owing to the fact that the client was feeling so much better, she was convinced that the doctor was going to take her off the medications but I informed her that the treatment would have to continue for much longer period than that. She told me that she heard that the treatment for the disease took six months and that she had completed over six months of therapy now and that she was feeling fine.

I picked up the client for the appointment as usual and the doctor decided to keep her on the medications for three months more. He also increased the dosage of medications that she was taking. The client was so much improved in weight that the M.D. prescribed the heavier dosage of medication, which he had restricted in the earlier stage, because at that time the client was so weak, and was weighing only 100 pounds.

After the client returned home with this new order of medications I discovered that she was very reluctant to take the tablets and I had to use a lot of persuasion in order for her to comply. After about four such visits I visited the client one evening for her usual Directly Observed Therapy and she was sitting outside with some friends and informed me to return at the appointed time the following afternoon, and she would take the pills.

Whenever situations like this occurred I always made sure to document it in the client's record using as much as possible the exact words that were spoken by the client. In addition I would inform both the nurse that was in charge of the tuberculosis clinic and the supervisor. I visited the client the following evening and as I knocked at the door for a few times, a lady opened the door and informed me that she was also visiting the client but that she wasn't there. I knew that the client was there, however, because I could hear the grumbling in her room. Well, I left a bit disappointed and returned the following day. The client's mother answered the door and informed me that the client was asleep but she would awaken her for me. I waited for some time and her mother returned and said the client answered but she refused to come out and take the medicines. I told her mother how important it was for her to take the medications until they were discontinued by the doctor. Her mother told me that she was pleased to see how much she had improved and that she encouraged her to continue taking the pills but she refused and said that she no longer had the disease. I returned to my office and wrote an account of the events, and informed my supervisor who instructed me that I should take the record to her so that she could have it reviewed by the Pulmonary Specialist who commented in his progress notes that the treatment was incomplete but the client was non-compliant and the record was closed on April 12,

1993. Now that the client had negative sputum and smears including the improvement in her chest x-rays the department could not have her committed at this stage. Although the case management of client "A" cannot be regarded as a complete story of success, I am justified that I did everything that was possible to enhance the recovery of this client and I was commended by all the parties involved for the part I played in helping to bring her recovery to that stage.

Client "B" continued on her Directly Observed Therapy despite the fact that she was absent on a few occasions. I began to receive complaints from the client that the medications were making her very sick. Since the client was taking a number of medications, only the M.D. could determine which of the medications were making her ill. I reported the matter to the tuberculosis monitor and she consulted with the physician about the side effects the client was experiencing. The client was given an appointment to see the Pulmonary Specialist and after examining her and reviewing her record, one of her medications was discontinued and she stated on future visits that she experienced those side effects no longer.

Due to the fact the client had prior treatment at A.G. Holly the duration of her Directly Observed therapy treatment at home was of a shorter duration. The client showed remarkable progress and eventually the doctor discontinued all her medications and gave her an appointment to return to the clinic within six months for a repeat chest x-ray. At the end of that period the client was examined and found to have no clinical tuberculosis. After clients are successfully treated, they are re-examined within six months to a year to make sure that there are no further infections.

Case III: "James Brown"

During the period of my training when I was taught how to review records, two clients were brought to my attention that were non-compliant and I was asked to endeavor to make home visits and try to get these clients into the clinic for treatment.

One of these clients was a black male in his early forties. I will list the client's name as "James Brown" for the purpose of not revealing his true identity. I visited the client at his home and gave him a brief lecture on tuberculosis transmission and control, and scheduled a clinic appointment for the client. The client had not been to the clinic for some time and he had no medications left. The client kept the appointment and he was placed on Directly Observed Therapy twice weekly. I worked out a schedule for the client and we agreed on Mondays and Fridays at 7:30 A.M. Although my hour of work was 8:00 A.M., I tried to be flexible and fit into this arrangement.

The client was compliant for a few weeks and then I began to miss him on a few occasions. I left messages with the client's sister and my phone number for the client to contact me at office or at home. The client called me at about 9:30 P.M. and informed me that he was engaged in some type of manual labor and he would like the schedule to be changed to 7:00 A.M. so that he could get to work on time. I learned then that although the client was seen at his sister's home and the Directly Observed Therapy was done there, the client lived at a different location, but he arranged to have all this done at his sister's home.

I discussed this time factor with my supervisor and she asked that I should enquire if the afternoon would be good for the client. The client informed me that he was off work late, and that only 6:00 P.M. would be good for him in the afternoon. I told my supervisor that I would fit him into the 7:00 A.M. schedule. I was an early riser anyway and I could be there at 7:00 A.M.

After this was agreed on the Directly Observed Therapy went on well for a few months and the client started complaining about some terrible itching he was experiencing. The matter was reported to the M.D. and the client was given an appointment to see him so that he could explain the side effects to the doctor himself. The doctor discontinued one of his medications, which he considered was causing the problem and replaced that medication with a new one. Fortunately the itching subsided and the client continued Directly Observed Therapy. This client was very non-compliant on previous occasions and sometimes would leave the clinic before he had even seen the doctor and received his medications. The nurse at the health center was not able to obtain a single sputum from him. Now that he was on Directly Observed Therapy, this was a relief for everyone.

The client was still not giving any sputum at the health center for bacteriological analysis and seldom would he allow his blood to be drawn S.G.O.T. (Serum Glutamic Oxal Axcetic Transaminase). The client now began to complain about the medications and started to question how long he would be taking them for. I told him that it was very essential for him to give sputums at the health center so that an analysis of his sputum could be made to see if the sputum had converted to negative. I also explained to him that the Pulmonary Specialist would be the one to determine when the medications were no longer required.

Shortly after, I began to miss the client on the 7:00 A.M. appointment. Whenever this happened I would leave a message to inform the client that I would return at 6:00 P.M., which was one of his aforementioned choices. Seldom would I see the client in the afternoon. He was always making excuses why he was unable to keep the appointments. I tried to educate him about how he could develop resistance to the disease if he did not comply and that it would be harder for him to be treated. The client promised to comply but eventually I could see him neither at the 7:00 A.M. appointment nor in the afternoon. His sister told me that she talked to him about complying with the Directly Observed Therapy but he failed to listen. She was also a trained health worker who worked at one of the hospitals and was quite aware of the nature of the disease and the consequences of not adhering to therapy.

After exploring all the available strategies I had to write a report of the client's non-compliance and submitted his record to the supervisor for review. His record was reviewed by the supervisor and the M.D. The M.D. was quite familiar of the problems associated with this client having dealt with him for a considerable period of time. At one stage he was even threatened by the specialist to be placed in the hospital at A.G. Holly but there was not sufficient evidence to have this client committed. They did not even have one positive sputum on him, which was taken at the health center. As a result of all these circumstances his record was closed stating that the client was non-compliant both for Directly Observed Therapy and at the health center also.

Case IV

This was the other case, which was referred to me for follow-up during my orientation on record review. This little boy was two years old and was diagnosed for Pulmonary Tuberculosis. His mother was very young and she failed to follow through with his treatment. My supervisor asked me to make this case a priority. I made home visits to the address on his record and found out that this was the home of his grandparents. The grandmother of the child told me that he was not living there and that the client was living with his mother. The grandmother was quite cooperative in accepting messages and appointments for the mother of the client but neither the address nor phone number of the client was disclosed.

I kept making home visits for several weeks, and leaving messages and appointment slips for the mother to take the child to the health center for continuation of treatment without any success. Each time the grandmother told me that she gave the message and delivered the appointment slips that I left. Despite all these disappointments I kept enquiring about the client until one day the mother of the client had to make a visit to the health center for some reason and the nurse that was in charge there got her phone number. I got the phone number and called the client's mother. At last I had an opportunity to talk with her and to impress on her the importance of taking the child to the health center to follow up on treatment. She assured me that she would keep the appointment that I gave her, but she did not. When I saw that she failed the appointment again, I telephoned her late that evening and had a brief discourse with her. I told her that I knew how much she loved her little boy but if she did not take him for treatment the disease would kill him and then she would have to live with that sad regret for the rest of her life, knowing that she could have prevented his death by getting the necessary treatment that could cure him. She told me that she would be taking the child to stay with his grandmother for some time and that the child could be seen there. I gave her an appointment right over the phone for the clinic.

At the next M.D.'s appointment, the first person to turn up with the child was the grandmother. The child was examined and placed on Directly Observed Therapy immediately. He was placed on INH and

Rifampin 150 mg each (liquid). His medication order requested Directly Observed Therapy daily from Mondays to Fridays and the parent or guardian should give the medications on Saturdays and Sundays. This was the first case I had to manage that required Directly Observed Therapy daily. The time schedule was worked out and the grandmother stated that 8:30 A.M. was a good time for her, but even if I made it at 8:00 A.M. that would still be all right. The medications ordered could not be obtained at the pharmacy at that health center so I volunteered to pick up the medications for them at a pharmacy, which was located at one of our other health centers that accommodated Medicaid. I picked up the medications late in the afternoon and the Directly Observed Therapy was started the following morning at 8:30. Sometimes when I made the home visit the client was still asleep, but the grandmother would have him awaken and prepared him for taking the medications. I informed her that I could rearrange the schedule for a later time since he was still asleep sometimes, but she assured me that the time was fine because she had to get ready for work on certain days. The grandmother of the client was a disciplinarian. She reminded me of my grandmother in some respects. She was a very sweet lady, but she was one who could let a child understand that she means business.

As I continued to visit this home for the Directly Observed Therapy I discovered that if the child was not staying with his grandmother it would almost be impossible to get him to take the medications. On Friday of the week which was my last day for Directly Observed Therapy for that week the grandmother told me that she would be going to a church convention over the weekend and would not return until later Monday afternoon, but the child's aunt would be there to give him the medications. When I arrived Monday morning the child's aunt called him for the medications. She had difficulty getting him to open his mouth for even the first teaspoonful. When she finally got the medications into his mouth, he kept it there but would not swallow it. He kept shaking his head in disapproval. She encouraged him, coaxed him, but he would not swallow the medications. Eventually she gave up and told me that she would give him the medications in some applesauce later, because she was out of applesauce at this time. I was alarmed at the change in this behavior of the client and left hoping that there would be a better response with the applesauce.

The following morning when I made the visit for the Directly Observed Therapy, the client's grandmother was home, and the client took the medications as easy as ABC. I informed the grandmother what had transpired the previous morning and she told me that children knew how to play games with certain people.

On another occasion, the grandmother was absent again for another day, and the mother of the child was present to give him the medications. She encountered a lot of problems doing this. It took her about a half an hour to get him to take the medications. I realized that maybe this was one of the reasons why she would not take the child to the health center to continue treatment, and why she finally decided to leave the child with his grandmother so that he could continue therapy. During this period that I had been visiting this home for the Directly Observed Therapy I was able to build good rapport with these people. The client himself seemed to have a liking for me. He was up and ready when I got there in the mornings and as I rang the buzzer, he came to get the door for me and ran to get his grandmother. He has gained weight and has shown such improvement that the doctor has given him clearance to go back to infant school.

He had completed six months of therapy and on his last M.D. appointment he was taken off Directly Observed Therapy by the doctor. The doctor asked me about the compliance and I was pleased to inform him that the grandmother of the client was very good at getting him to take the medications. She could really get him to understand. I told him that it was a pleasure to work with such nice people for a change who are so cooperative.

Whenever his medications were getting low, the grandmother of the client would give me a call at the health center and I would get the tuberculosis monitor to call in the prescription at the pharmacy. I then picked up the medications and delivered it to the grandmother of the client with instructions.

On the client's last M.D. appointment, the M.D. was pleased with the progress that the client has made, and he has been given another month to continue medications at the end of which period the M.D. will see him again. I am confident that the M.D. will discontinue medications on this visit hoping that everything will be all right. I will regard this as a triumph when this phase of treatment is finally completed.

Case V: "George"

One of the responsibilities of the Health Services Representative is to make a home/hospital visit within two working days of receipt of "Interoffice Communications on New Patients." Whenever a patient is admitted to the hospital and a chest x-ray is taken, if the chest x-ray is abnormal, an Interoffice communication is sent to the health department so that a visit can be made to the home of the client and an appointment can be made for the client to attend the health center so that a chest x-ray can be repeated. Some of these clients are just examined in the Emergency Room and sent home.

If the client is diagnosed for Mycobacterium tuberculosis while in the hospital, the health department is notified, and if the client is in the hospital for a while, a home visit will be made to the hospital to interview the client and get all necessary information prior to the client's release.

In case number five, a client, black male, aged 47 years was admitted to the hospital and diagnosed for Mycobacterium tuberculosis. A public health nurse was assigned this case and she made several visits and scheduled clinic appointments for the client who promised her faithfully that he would attend the health center but each time he failed to turn up for treatment. The nurse became frustrated and told the tuberculosis monitor that she had no success with the client and was asking her if she could assign the case to another health worker. This nurse was highly spoken of as one of the best on the health team and no one else wanted to tackle a case that she was unsuccessful with.

The tuberculosis monitor told me that she was asking me to make a home visit and give the client an appointment for the health center. I made a visit to the client's apartment but I did not see the client. I did not know the client either, so that I could identify him if I had seen him outside. As I was returning to my car I saw a gentleman sitting outside and I asked him if he knew the client. (I will list the client's name as George so as not to reveal the client's true identity). He told me that he did not know the client of whom I enquired. He had a wry smile on his face and I walked back to my car. As I opened the car door I had a hunch about this guy and I walked back to him and said "Are you sure that you don't know George, I just want to give him an appointment for the clinic." He laughed and I said "You are George, aren't you?" and he nodded. I gave him a brief talk about tuberculosis and impressed on him in simple language the importance of attending the health center to receive treatment for the disease before it killed him. I also gave him an appointment for the clinic.

On the day of the appointment, no one believed that the client would turn up after failing those previous appointments but he did. The doctor placed him on Directly Observed Therapy Mondays through Fridays and he was allowed to take the treatment on his own on Saturdays and Sundays. This was the second case of a daily Directly Observed Therapy client that was assigned to me.

I visited the client's home for the Directly Observed Therapy and discovered that there were a lot of other people living in the apartment. The client was unable to open the bottles with the medications and I spent some time showing this client how to open these bottles since he would be taking the medicines on his own on Saturdays and Sundays. It took a few days before the client mastered the simple technique to push down and turn. Although this client was not an arthritis sufferer, if left to him this could easily result in non-compliance. The client agreed on an 8:30 A.M. appointment and he was fairly compliant for the first two months. He admitted on a few occasions that he had forgotten to take the medications on weekends; however, I told him how important it was for him to take these medications on a daily basis. There was an elderly gentleman also living in the apartment and he promised that he would remind him to take his pills on weekends.

George did well on his medications for the first few months. Rarely did I miss him on a visit for Directly Observed Therapy and if I did miss him I would make a revisit to try and locate him. Sometimes when I did not find the client at home, I was told that he could be found at the next door's neighbor's house.

George also liked his beer and occasionally I could see him dodging away that beer can when I arrived. Despite his occasional drinking, the client was not boisterous and he never refused to take his medicines when I arrived.

One of the main problems encountered with George was that he would frequently miss the doctor's appointment. Although he does not own any transportation for himself, he had friends who could take him to the clinic. Sometimes when my schedule afforded me the time, I would take him to the clinic myself. I also gave him bus tokens whenever it was needed.

The M.D. discontinued the Directly Observed Therapy about three months ago and George is now allowed to take the medicines on his own. I frequently make home visits to see if he is complying with the Doctor's order and to reinforce the importance of staying on the medications until treatment is completed.

On George's recent visit to the Doctor, he was given two months more to continue medications, at the end of which he will have an M.D. evaluation which will determine if he will be off medications completely. He is the type of client who needs supervision until treatment is completed. By that I mean that even though he is no longer on Directly Observed Therapy, he needs to be visited at frequent intervals to make sure that he is complying on his own.

Case VI: "Jane"

This is a lady who has a history of tuberculosis in her family. Her mother was treated for tuberculosis previously and has had history of non-compliance. Owing to the past family history, on her first visit to the doctor, after she was diagnosed for tuberculosis she was ordered to be on Directly Observed Therapy daily by the physician. This client lived in the same apartment complex that George lived in. There was also a problem sometimes in awakening her and sometimes I would have to make a return visit in order to see her take the pills. This client, whose name I will just mention as "Jane" told me some mornings that she was not feeling well to take the tablets at that time, but she would take them later. I had to find out what time she believed she would take them and then make a later visit for Directly Observed Therapy.

As previously stated, when you are dealing with Directly Observed Therapy clients you have to adjust the schedule from time to time. If a client states that he or she is not feeling well at the moment it is not appropriate to force the client to take the medications at that time, so it's better to arrange a time for a later visit. The client could be sincere in stating that he or she is not feeling well. On the other hand, the client could be using this as a strategy not to take the tablets. If this strategy is used successfully by the client two or three times, the health worker could lose control of this Directly Observed Therapy client.

Jane also would be absent occasionally on the visits for Directly Observed Therapy. Although our scheduled time was 8:00 A.M., we had to adjust the schedule sometimes to 11:00 A.M. Whenever Jane was absent when I saw her the other day, she would inform me that she had to take her child to the doctor and that she had another appointment with Social Services or something else.

She had no problem with the taking of the medications whenever I arrived. She also assured me that if she was absent one day she always took the tablets because she wanted to get well. Jane also had two teenagers who frequently used drugs and sometimes they were caught and taken to jail by the police. Whenever this occurred, for instance, on a morning before her medications were taken, she told me that she was upset and would ask me to return later to see her take her medications.

Two of her children had positive reactions to the PPD test but their chest x-rays were all right. Both of them were placed on INH Preventive Therapy for six months with daily intake of Isoniazid. The younger child completed his six months of therapy. The elder child, after receiving his first set of medications never returned to the clinic. He was one who was involved in drugs and his mother could not seem to control him.

Whenever she was getting low on medications before another M.D. visit was due, I would ask the tuberculosis monitor to order her medications and I would take them to her. She rarely missed a doctor's visit although she did not have transportation of her own. Bus tokens were frequently provided and sometimes she would be taken to the health center by a friend.

After she completed six months of Directly Observed Therapy her condition was so improved that she was allowed to take medications on her own. Each time the client attends the health center certain tests are performed to detect if any of the medications are causing any harm. One of these tests is called SGOT (Serum Glutamic Oxal Acetic Transaminase). This is an enzyme, which is found in the heart muscle or liver. On one of these tests, Jane was found to have a high SGOT. Further studies were done and her medications were discontinued. She had negative x-rays prior to that and the M.D. indicated that there was no further evidence of the disease.

Case VII: "Jay"

Black male aged 37 years. He was admitted to the hospital and was diagnosed positive for Mycobacterium tuberculosis. During his hospital stay he was placed in isolation for a brief period. An interoffice Communication was received from the hospital prior to his discharge and I was instructed to make a home visit and elicit the contacts.

After the client was discharged from the hospital, I made a home visit and interviewed the client. He was extremely weak and thin, and he also complained that he had a fever. In addition to the treatments he had taken home with him from the hospital he also had a special type of medication (tagament) for stomach trouble, which he encountered. The physician that attended the client in the hospital recommended that he should be placed on Directly Observed Therapy due to the seriousness of his illness. I discussed the transmission and control of tuberculosis with the client and his family members. The family members were already aware that he had tuberculosis. In addition to the contact worksheet, which was already completed, a Multi-drug Risk Assessment Form was also completed. This form had the questions, which the client would answer yes, or no. these questions are listed below:

(1) Are you under 18 years old?
(2) Have you ever been treated for tuberculosis in the past?
(3) Have you ever been treated with INH preventative therapy?
(4) Were you ever exposed to someone who had Multi-drug Resistant Tuberculosis?
(5) Do you drink wine, beer, or mixed drinks on a regular basis?
(6) Have you ever used drugs such as crack or heroine?
(7) Have you ever been told that you tested positive for HIV infection or AIDS?
(8) Were you born in, or have you ever lived in Asia, Africa or Latin America?
(9) Have you ever lived in New York?
(10) Do you have any problems, which make it difficult for you to take your medication on a daily basis?

After giving the answers to these questions, the patient would be asked to sign his or her name after which the Health Services Representative would also sign his or her name and date the form. This along with the episodic notes would be turned in to the appropriate supervisor for correct routing. The MDR Risk Assessment Tool enables one to make a quick evaluation of some of the behavior of the client.

After the lecture on tuberculosis and the completion of the necessary forms the client was given an appointment to see the Pulmonary Specialist. On the day of his appointment, the client complained that he was feeling so bad that they had to make an exception to the general rule "first come first serve" and get him in to see the doctor. The specialist placed the client on D.O.T as was previously recommended. This client whose name I will call "Jay" was cooperative in taking his medicine. He was asleep a few times when I got there, but his mother did not encounter a problem in waking him.

During the first few weeks the client still had a fever, but gradually the fever left him. In the weeks ahead his stomach problem also improved. The client also stated that his appetite had improved but he was still weak and spent most of the time sleeping. The client's mother was very attentive to his needs and it was observed during home visits that a close family relationship existed. It appeared that clients' recoveries are more expedient when they have support of their family and friends. The client also had a daughter about ten years old who was living in the home and she was given a PPD test along with the other family members who were contacts and they were all found negative.

The client's M.D. order for Directly Observed Therapy was twice weekly. I scheduled the time for 8:00 A.M. on Tuesdays and Fridays. During the first three months of Directly Observed Therapy administration the client was always found at home. Sometimes after knocking at the door for a long time, I would leave and make a return visit in the afternoon. The client always left his radio on when he fell asleep and it was impossible for him to hear anything that was going on in the outside world.

Due to the fact that the client had a history of drug use, it was argued that he might not be compliant. However, the client was compliant so far with the exception of missing a few M.D. appointments. The client informed me that when he attended the health center he had to wait so long to see the M.D. and that he was not feeling well. He informed me that sitting up for a long time made him exhausted and he wanted to lie down. This problem was overcome by giving the client an earlier appointment and asked him to reach the health center so that he would be the first one to sign in. Clients are provided with a signing sheet at the health center on which the client signs his name and the time. They are usually called in the order in which they sign in, unless it is a case of emergency. A quick glance at the signing sheet reveals which client has not turned up for the appointment.

As "Jay" continued therapy, he gradually gained strength, and his complaints about weakness have disappeared. The chest x-rays taken have showed remarkable improvement and his sputum were converted to negative. After the client had completed six months of therapy, he was taken off Directly Observed Therapy and allowed to take the medications on his own. The client was very happy, likewise his mother who promised that she would be sure to see him take the medications in case he had forgotten.

The last time the client was evaluated by the M.D., he was given three months to return to the clinic for x-rays and medical review. The client failed to keep the appointment although I reminded him by telephone just the day prior to the appointment. I rescheduled another appointment for the client so that he could have his medications refilled. On the day of the appointment, the client was not present at 12:00 P.M. so I gave him another call and he told me that he was on his way. The client attended the health center and was seen by the tuberculosis monitor and his medications refilled.

The client was scheduled another M.D.'s appointment since no M.D. was available on that date. The client missed the M.D. appointment again. I made a home visit just the day before the appointment and reminded the client personally about the appointment. The client showed me where he had placed the written appointment that was given to him. The appointment was posted right on his almanac. With all these reminders, the client failed to keep the M.D.'s appointment again. I gave him a call the day after and he informed me that he had an appointment somewhere and was not able to make it back on time. He did inform me, however, that he had only one dose of medications left so I asked the nurse to call in the refill on his medications and I took the medications to him.

Sometimes we are amazed at the behavior of these clients. We would consider that after a client had completed about nine months of therapy that the client would be eager to attend the health center to have his case reviewed by the specialist so that his medications can be discontinued but this was not the case with this client.

Despite all this, I kept visiting the client and made sure that he had medications on hand until finally I got him to keep his M.D.'s appointment. I visited his home the morning before the appointment and reminded him again. His mother told me that she would make sure that he was there on that day. His interview with the specialist went well and he was taken off all his medications. His next follow-up was due in twelve months.

The following cases, which I will relate, take on different perspectives, some of them are multi-drug resistant, and others are grossly non-compliant. All but one shares one thing in common however, in the cases that I shall relate, the clients are infected with the Human Immunodeficiency Virus.

Case VIII

This client was a black female, aged about sixty years old. She had various ailments of which the two most severe were tuberculosis and AIDS. She was admitted to the hospital several times, and was treated and sent home to continue further treatment. The specialist at the health center ordered Directly Observed Therapy three times weekly. Streptomycin was included in the medication regime.

The client was compliant in attending the health center three times weekly as was ordered. After a good period had elapsed the streptomycin was discontinued and the client was allowed to take her medications on her own at home.

After the client continued therapy for a reasonable period of time, she became ill and was admitted to the hospital again. The client spent several weeks in the hospital and a number of bacteriological tests were performed and it was discovered that the client was resistant to INH, Rifampin and PZA. INH (Isoniazid) and Rifampin are two of the principal drugs in treating tuberculosis and whenever the client is resistant to these drugs, second-class drugs are used which are less effective. In addition, whenever a patient is infected with the HIV virus, the tuberculosis is more difficult to be treated and takes a much longer time.

After the client was released from the hospital, she moved to a different location to stay with a relative. It took a while before this new location was found. When the client was finally located, two of the medications that she was taking were finished and I reported this to the Community Health Nursing Supervisor who instructed that I would take the client's record for review by the M.D. The medical record was reviewed and the prescriptions were filled and taken to the client. The client was extremely grateful for the medications when I delivered them to her.

The client had no telephone where she was living and so I had to make frequent home visits to enquire how well she was doing. On my last visit the client was sitting outside talking with some friends and she remarked that she was doing much better. She was scheduled an M.D.'s appointment in two weeks. Her son assured me that he would take her to the health center at the appointed time. The client did not turn up for her appointment however. I made a home visit the following day but no one was seen at home. Another visit was made in about three days and the client's relatives told me that she was feeling so well that she went to visit her daughter in another state. I was unable to get the address and the name of the relative with whom she was staying.

I made another home visit in about two weeks and enquired if she had returned and I was informed by the relatives that the client expired and they had returned from the funeral the previous day. I gathered all the necessary information about the name of the relative and the location in Pennsylvania where the client resided prior to her expiration, and furnished the information to the health department so that the department of health in that state could be contacted and notify the contacts for examination. The contacts in our area were investigated and given the appropriate test.

Case IX "Cathy"

This is a young lady in her early twenties that was diagnosed positive for Mycobacterium tuberculosis and also HIV. She was hospitalized for an infection that she had in her finger. She is a drug user, and she smokes and also drinks a lot of alcohol.

She was discharged from the hospital and was placed under the supervision of a Public Health Nurse who made daily visits to treat her finger, which was in the process of healing. She was also ordered Directly Observed Therapy by the specialist for tuberculosis. The client was living at one of those rental apartments with other relatives. On the first day I visited the client she was still asleep. It was about 10:30 A.M. and I told the relatives that I was there to see the client whose name I will list as "Cathy". A relative went to awaken the client and it took about twenty minutes after battering the door before the client came out of the apartment. I wondered what my subsequent visits would be like.

I explained the Directly Observed Therapy procedure to the client and observed her take her first dosage of medications. She told me that 10:30 A.M. was fine for her. She was ordered Directly Observed Therapy twice weekly. Mondays and Thursdays were the days, which we agreed on. When I went back at 10:30 A.M. the Thursday morning, someone went to get the client again; I waited about ten minutes before the client came out. I considered that to be a great improvement considering the time I waited on the first visit. The client took her medications and returned to sleep.

On my third visit, after the client was awakened, I was told to go into her apartment to see her take the medications. The client had come into the living area prior to that to take her medications. When I entered the apartment, the client had gone back to sleep. I had to call her several times before she finally got out of the bed. The client stumbled around her apartment for a while before she could locate her medications. It took her also a good period of time to get some water to take the medications. I always carried paper bags in my car so I got one and placed all the Tuberculosis medicines in it and asked the client to keep it in a special place where it could be easily found. The client also had other medications for the HIV, which she was not required to take under supervision but she always took those medications also on arrival.

The client was also given an appointment to see the tuberculosis specialist at the health center and three sputum containers for the collection of specimens. The client failed to keep the clinic appointment but she did collect the sputum, which I picked up and returned to the health center. This sputum was sent to the bacteriological laboratory for analysis.

The Directly Observed Therapy continued for about three months. Sometimes other relatives were not present and I encountered great difficulties getting this client to awaken for her medications. When the client awoke, I had to keep calling her to prevent her from going back to sleep before taking the medications. There was no improvement in this particular behavior of the client. It made me frustrated sometimes but I realized that there would be difficult situations and I just had to cope with it.

One day I went for the Directly Observed Therapy and I knocked at her door for some time and got no response. A relative of hers came to my rescue, battered the door and called her name until he got the door opened, but "Cathy" was not to be found in her room. I left a message with the relative that I would return later. When I returned I saw "Cathy" and she told me that she had to leave at 5:00 A.M. to see her father who was ill and she had taken the medications already. I told her that it was important that I saw her take these medications, and that I could adjust the schedule if that time was not alright for her. She said that the time was OK.

I made several other visits for Directly Observed Therapy and "Cathy" could not be found. Sometimes, I was told by her relatives that she had just gone to the store. I left messages for her but I got no response. One day I went to see her and I was told that she was at a friend's home which was close by. I went to the friend's home and found her drinking beer with her friends. I called her aside and had a good discussion with her about the disease, and the importance of the Directly Observed Therapy. She told me that she was taking the medications and that she did not have to be seen by someone to take them. A full report on the matter was submitted to the supervisor and the record was given to the M.D. for review who discontinued the Directly Observed Therapy and instructed that she should take the medications on her own.

Several appointments were given to her for the clinic, but she never kept one of those appointments. I continued to take sputum containers to her for the collection of sputum and she was quite cooperative in this area. I also made home visits and checked her compliance with the medications. I took new medicines to her when her supply of medications was near completion.

Several visits have been made accompanied by the tuberculosis monitor and other field nurses. Bus tokens have been given to her and she has been offered rides to the health center but she always gives us excuses about why she is unable to attend. Cathy is well known for her non-compliance. The only good thing so far is that all her sputum results from the bacteriological laboratory recently have been found negative. No chest x-rays have been taken at the health center so far because she never attends the center. We still make home visits and refill her medications when necessary. Her case is still open and we will have to endure with her non-compliance and continue to treat her for her own good and the good of the community. That is all we can do for now because since "Cathy's" sputum's are negative, the Department cannot have her court committed to A.G. Holly.

Case X: "Allan"

The client whom I will refer to as "Allan" is a black male. The client was diagnosed for pulmonary tuberculosis and AIDS at the local hospital. His case was assigned to one of the Public Health Nurses for follow-up after he was discharged from the hospital. The nurse made several home visits but the client was not contacted. Within a short period of time information was received that the client was re-admitted to the hospital. The physician that was attending him at the hospital recommended Directly Observed Therapy. As the client's condition improved a little at the hospital, the client walked out of the hospital before he was discharged. The health department was contacted and I was assigned this client's case for follow-up and the Directly Observed Therapy.

I visited the home a few times and knocked at the door, but I got no response. One day I visited the home early in the morning and as I knocked at the door, I got a faint response from inside. I kept calling the client by name and I identified myself but there was no further response of anyone. Subsequent visits were made without any sign of success, until late one evening I made a visit and low and behold the client's door was opened and he was lying in his bed. A lady was living in the apartment with the client who told me that she left for work about 5:00 A.M.

I tried to interview the client but he was so weak the lady had to help him up out of bed and he only nodded to some of the questions that I asked him. The lady who was his supposed spouse answered the rest of the questions however.

The client had some tuberculosis medications along with those for the HIV infection. The lady told me that his last meal was eaten the day before, and she prepared meals since then but he had not eaten. She was extremely concerned about him. I collected the old tuberculosis medicines and took them back to the department and a new order of medication was filled.

When I went back the following afternoon with the new order of medications for the Directly Observed Therapy no one was seen at home. There was no phone at the home by which the client could be contacted, and the only time I could see the lady was in the evening since she went to work at 5:00 A.M. I paid a visit the following evening at 3:30 P.M. and the lady told me that he was admitted to another hospital this time.

Well this was good news to me and I just told the lady I would keep checking until he returned from the hospital. I also completed the worksheet for the contacts and discovered that the client was the father of a two-year-old girl of which this lady was the mother. She was also given an appointment to attend the health center with the child for a PPD test.

The administration of Directly Observed Therapy was a very difficult process from even the first dosage of medication. The client kept saying, "I am not going to take it". However, with the persuasion of his lady the Directly Observed Therapy continued for two weeks. Although the client agreed at 3:00 P.M., after the first three visits he told me that I was not going to find him there sometimes, because he was there alone, and sometimes he would be gone somewhere else. The client meant every word that he said. After two weeks of Directly Observed Therapy I made a visit at the usual hour and the client was not there. The lady told me that she did not see him when she returned from work. Apparently he had someone picked him up and he did not return for the Directly Observed Therapy. On two subsequent visits the lady was absent and he told me bluntly that he was not going to take the medicines, and that he did not know where the lady had placed them. I looked around the apartment until I found the medicines. I counted the dosage of tablets and placed them in the client's hand. The client just let the tablets fall out of his hand and said that he was not going to take the tablets.

Each time I documented the client's non-compliant behavior. He was also educated several times about the transmission of the disease and that he needed to take these medicines in order to get better. The client told me that if he had tuberculosis he would not be released from the hospital but he would be confined there with a mask over his face. I wrote down everything that he said in his medical record. A visit was also made with the tuberculosis monitor but this client listened to no one. I scheduled an M.D. appointment for him and he was taken to the health center by his lady to see the specialist. The specialist told him after reviewing his x-ray that he would recommend that he be sent to A.G. Holly unless he decided to continue the Directly Observed

Therapy. The client told the M.D. that he did not want anyone to come and see him take his medicine and that he would rather kill himself than to be admitted to A.G. Holly Hospital. The client's lady assured the doctor that she would endeavor to get him to take the medications. He was sent home with the medications to be given by his lady friend.

After this I made another home visit to pick up some sputum containers for the client. These were submitted for bacteriological analysis. Two weeks after this the client expired. Allan can be regarded as one of the most non-compliant cases I have ever encountered. His record was reviewed by the M.D. and closed.

Cases XI: "Larry

The client was a black male in his early twenties and he was diagnosed for Mycobacterium tuberculosis in the stool and he was also HIV positive. I made a home visit after receiving an "Interoffice Communication" on this client. The interview went on quite smoothly. Tuberculosis education was given to the client and his family. The client resided with his relatives and they were very concerned about his health status. The services of the health department were offered and the client decided that he wanted to attend the health center for treatment since he did not have a private physician.

The form for Multi-drug resistant tuberculosis was completed and the worksheet for contacts was also completed. There were about ten persons living in this home with the client. The client was scheduled an appointment to see the M.D. at the health center. After completing the reports I turned them over to the tuberculosis monitor and these reports became a part of his record.

When the client was examined by the specialist he was ordered Directly Observed Therapy three times weekly. Streptomycin was included in his medication regime and since he had to attend the health center three times weekly for the streptomycin shot his other medications were also given at the same time, and observed by the nurse who gave the injections.

The client was compliant for about three months and then I was informed by the nurse at the health center that she did not see the client for about a week. I telephoned his home but there was no response. I also made home visits but no one was there whenever I visited the home. I left a written appointment at the door and a card with my office number for the client to contact me but I got no response from him. Finally I got a call from the client's mother stating that he left home for about two weeks and she did not know where to contact him. The client came to the health center accompanied by his mother the following week. "Larry" had driven to New York, Washington DC and some other places. The client was mobile and he was touring the states.

Shortly after this he was admitted to the local hospital and he was treated and sent home. He had a stroke after he was released from the hospital, and his mother informed us by telephone that he was so ill that she could not take him to the clinic to receive the streptomycin and other medications. The tuberculosis monitor and I took the medications to his home. The streptomycin was administered by a health care worker from the Hospice Department and I had to make home visits for the Directly Observed Therapy. The tablets that he was taking had to be crushed and given to him in applesauce.

The last day I visited him for Directly Observed Therapy he was so ill that he could not take the medications. His mother assured me that she would endeavor to see if he could take the medications later.

The following day I called to find out how "Larry" was doing and his mother informed me that he expired the previous day after I left in the afternoon.

Since then, the tuberculosis monitor made arrangements to have the PPD testing of the contacts done in the home since there were so many people living there. We were able to accomplish this a few weeks ago. Fortunately all the contacts tested were found negative.

Case XII: "Ellis"

This client was admitted to the Emergency Room of the local hospital as a result of a stomach problem and was treated and sent home.

An "Interoffice Communication" was received by the Department depicting an abnormal chest x-ray and I made a home visit to interview the client and schedule an appointment for a repeat chest x-ray. On my arrival at the home, the client was not there, and his mother told me that he did not live there but he had his meals there. She sent someone to call the client who was not staying that far away.

On the client's arrival, he told me that he was not admitted to the hospital because there were insufficient beds, but he might return for admittance at a later date. He had a bottle of tablets, which he was taking for his stomach condition.

The client was given a brief interview and an appointment was scheduled for the health center so that his chest x-ray would be repeated and reviewed by the specialist. The client assured me that he would attend the health center at the appointed time but he did not show up on the date given. Another visit was made to see the client again, but the client was not seen and a written appointment was left with his mother for him to attend the health center for the repeat chest x-ray.

Before the date of his appointment the client was admitted to the hospital. He was in the hospital for a good time and had surgery of the pancreas. He was diagnosed positive for Mycobacterium tuberculosis of the gastrointestinal tract and he was ordered Directly Observed Therapy on his discharge from the hospital.

The client was visited at his home by the tuberculosis monitor and myself. His record was opened and the list of medicines he was taken was noted. During the multi-drug report questioning, the client also admitted that he was HIV positive. I explained the Directly Observed Therapy procedure to the client. His Directly Observed Therapy order was daily with the exceptions of Saturdays and Sundays when he would take the medications on his own. The hour of 9:00 A.M. daily was agreed on for the Directly Observed Therapy. The client took his medications the first day without any problem but after that it was a problem every day.

The client was asleep many times when I arrived for the Directly Observed Therapy and he always complained that he was very weak. He never took his medications without a long discourse. He always complained that he was feeling bad and would like to take the medications later. Knowing the seriousness of his illness, I persuaded him to take the medications. On two occasions the client appeared to be experiencing a lot of pains and his mother assured me that she would see to it that he took the medication if the pains subsided. The last time I visited the client, his mother told me that he was not doing well, and I advised her to try and get him back to the hospital. He took the medications but he was extremely weak. This was on Friday of the week and I would not see the client again until the following Monday.

When I made a home visit on the Monday, his mother told me that she took him to the hospital about 5:00 P.M. on the previous Friday and he was re-admitted to the hospital. I kept in touch with his mother to find out how he was doing in the hospital and she informed me that his condition was deteriorating.

After about three weeks in the hospital, his condition improved and he was transferred to another hospital. He remained there for two weeks and his condition worsened and he died. I received the information when I made a home visit to enquire about him. His mother was very mournful and told me that this was the second son she lost who was infected with the AIDS virus. She told me that both of her sons who died were involved in drugs on the street using needles etc. I tried to console her and relayed the information to the Department for his record to be reviewed and closed.

Case XIII: "Rosie"

This client was diagnosed for Mycobacterium tuberculosis and also was infected with the HIV virus. The client was visited at home by the tuberculosis monitor and myself after she was released from the hospital. After the interview was conducted, the client was educated about tuberculosis transmission and how it can be controlled. The client was also informed about the HIV virus and the importance of taking the medications as prescribed.

The client was also informed that she was ordered Directly Observed Therapy daily with the exception of Saturdays and Sundays when she would take the medications on her own.

The client agreed on the 9:30 A.m. appointment. She was also given an appointment to attend the health center at a later date for an M.D. evaluation. The client was also informed that due to the nature of her illness, she would have to attend another health center too, where she should be given additional treatment for the HIV.

The clients Directly Observed Therapy supervision began on a Wednesday and things went smoothly for that week. On the following Monday when I arrived at the client's home, no one responded. I made a visit later in the afternoon but the client was absent also.

On the following day when I made the home visit, the client was present and I spent some time explaining to the client that she must be present for the Directly Observed Therapy daily and if a change of schedule was necessary, she should inform me. The client assured me that she would be present for the Directly Observed Therapy on a daily basis.

She continued the Directly Observed Therapy for a week without missing any of the scheduled appointments and then the following week she was absent on the Friday. The client gave no advance notice that she was going to be absent. When I saw her on Monday of the next week, she told me that she did not take the medicine because she had to visit her mother on that day.

The client also missed her appointment on the first day she was scheduled to see the specialist. She explained the following day that she was mistaken about the appointment and attended the wrong health center. When the error was discovered, it was too late to attend the health center for which she was scheduled to see the M.D.

Since then, arrangements have been worked out so that clients can receive treatment at this Special Health Center for both tuberculosis and HIV so that clients can be better accommodated. One of the disadvantages of the Special Health Center for the HIV clients is due to the fact that a pharmacy is not located at this center and sometimes the clients have to pick up some of their medications at the main facility. Despite this limitation, however, this clinic works out better for patients that are both HIV positive and tuberculosis patients.

"Rosie" has been on Directly Observed Therapy for about two months now. She still misses a day sometimes out of a week, but she said that whenever this happens she always takes her medications. The client is only taking three different medications for tuberculosis at this time. The client expressed that she is feeling better, but she will have to remain taking these medications for a good length of time before complete recovery of the tuberculosis is attained. "Rosie" was a user of drugs and alcohol, but she admitted that she no longer uses drugs. Many HIV infected patients have acquired the disease through the use of drugs, especially using needles. This client will continue to be monitored under Directly Observed Therapy until the MD considers that the client no longer requires such supervision.

Case XIV: "Cheri"

This client was diagnosed for Mycobacterium tuberculosis in the hospital and is also HIV positive. She was ordered Directly Observed Therapy shortly after her discharge from the hospital.

On the client's release from the hospital, I made a home visit and completed the rest of my reports by interviewing the client and educating the client and family members about tuberculosis. The client had some prescriptions, which were already filled. Those prescriptions, which were not filled for the tuberculosis medications, were taken to the tuberculosis monitor and ordered from the pharmacy and then taken to the client.

The client gave me a new address to which she should be moving the next day on which the Directly Observed Therapy should be started. We agreed on a 10:00 A.M. appointment and the Directly Observed Therapy was ordered twice weekly. Directly Observed Therapy was conducted for three weeks without much difficulty. There was some difficulty in getting the client to awaken sometimes but there was no problem getting the client to take the medications. The days for the Directly Observed Therapy were Mondays and Thursdays. During the fourth week I could not locate the client. I made two visits on Monday but there was no response from the client. I called and I knocked at the door, but no one answered. I left a note at the door of the client that I would return the following morning. The client had no telephone and so she could not be contacted unless by a home visit. Home visits were made on Tuesdays and Wednesdays also, but the client was not seen. On the Thursday, which was the normal day for the Directly Observed Therapy, I made a home visit and contacted the manager of the apartment to find out if she had moved. The manager informed me that the client was given notice to leave the apartment because she would not pay her rent. He told me that the client had not paid any rent for about two months. He opened the door of the apartment and the only things that were in the apartment were two bundles of clothes, which were tied up.

I reported the matter to the supervisor and submitted a report to the department stating that the client had moved and left no forwarding address. Later on, I made some home visits to the grandmother's home to see if she returned there. Her grandmother told me that she had the rental apartment before she was hospitalized and that she was just staying with her one day after she was released from the hospital. The grandmother said that she was the one who cared for the children. Several attempts were made to locate the client but they were unsuccessful. One day I saw the grandmother at the clinic with the children and she told me that the client was caught stealing and was arrested and incarcerated at one of the county jails. Provision is made for clients to be treated for infectious diseases during the period of which they are incarcerated.

All the contacts of the client have been given PPD test and are found negative. Reports from the laboratory of the client's sputum are also negative. The client was released from the County Jail about a month ago. On notification of her release, I heard that she was staying at her grandmother's home. Three home visits have been made and the client was given appointments to attend the health center for medical evaluation and for continuation of therapy but the client failed to keep any of the appointments. I contacted the grandmother of the client by phone recently and she informed me that the client was no longer there. I consulted with the nursing supervisor who advised that the necessary episodic notes should be written and the record to be taken to the M.D. for review.

Case XV: "Sonny"

An Interoffice Communication was received from the local hospital that this client was hospitalized and diagnosed for pulmonary tuberculosis. The client was also infected with the AIDS virus. Contact investigations of the client's friends were done and they were given PPD skin test. Only one of the tests turned out positive but the lady informed us later on that she had a previous history of positive PPD tests. If this information was relayed earlier on, she would never be given a skin test again because once you have a positive skin test the future test will always be positive. She was scheduled for a chest x-ray at the health center and the chest x-ray was found negative.

The client remained in the local hospital for about two months and then he was transferred to the A.G. Holly Hospital where the tuberculosis clients are hospitalized and treated. Many clients completed therapy there and have no need to take any more medicines when they are discharged. When "Sonny" was discharged, however, he was asked to continue therapy for about three more months. The M.D. ordered Directly Observed Therapy for the client twice weekly.

I was informed that the client would be staying at his mother's home, but on my arrival at the home, the client's mother told me that he was not living there but he visited her occasionally and maybe he gave the Department her phone number since he did not have a phone where he was living. The client's correct address was given and I made a visit to his apartment at about 4:45 pm. The client had a lady friend living in the apartment with him and he informed me that his health was greatly improved. I checked his medications and found out that he had only two doses of each medication left and that a new order of medication was required.

Directly Observed Therapy was discussed with the client, and the days of Monday and Thursday were agreed on at 9:00 am. The client had complied with the Directly Observed Therapy on the days scheduled and he had never missed a scheduled appointment for the Directly Observed Therapy but the client failed to attend the health center for his M.D. evaluations. The client has been provided with bus tokens for travelling to the health center but he complains that sometimes it's rainy and he does not want to get pneumonia. Sometimes he said that he overslept.

He has been assigned to the Special Clinic so that he can receive medical attention there for the HIV and other ailments other than tuberculosis. He complains that he has to travel a long distance to the main pharmacy to pick up his other prescriptions. He attends the Special Clinic because he is just living a few chains away. Arrangements have been made for the client to receive all the medical attention both for the HIV and Tuberculosis at the Special Clinic. The M.D. at this Special Clinic has also extended his period of treatment for tuberculosis for two more months.

Whenever a client is transferred to the Special Clinic, all the client's records are also transferred to this center. There is now a Health Service Representative, which has recently been assigned to this Special Health Center. I have also transferred the client's responsibility for D.O.T to the newly assigned Health Service Representative as of March 3, 1994. The new H.S.R has been officially introduced to the client who is now under her supervision.

Case XVI: "Harry"

This client was admitted to the local hospital and was diagnosed for Mycobacterium tuberculosis and is also infected with the HIV virus. On his discharge from the hospital, the client was interviewed in the usual manner and given an appointment for the health center to be evaluated by the Pulmonary Specialist. It was observed that the client was running low on two of his medications and this was reported to the tuberculosis monitor and the prescriptions were filled and taken to him.

The client was also given an appointment to attend the Special Health Center, which was now taking care of the clients who were HIV infected. This appointment was for a later date after the Pulmonary Specialist was seen.

The client kept his M.D. appointment and he was the first client to be present and seen by the Pulmonary Specialist. The client was ordered D.O.T daily. The arrangements were worked out with him at the clinic and the hour of 8:00 AM was agreed on.

The following morning I made the visit at 7:50 AM. I decided that I would just wait for ten minutes but the client was waiting for me. Two of his capsules should be taken on an empty stomach and the client had those taken already, and he had eaten and had the rest of his tablets counted and placed in a little dish. The client took his medicine joyfully. I have not remembered anyone so jubilant in taking his or her medications. The client placed all the tablets in his mouth at the same time and just swallowed them down with water.

Each day that I went for the D.O.T, the client was ready and waiting. He made no hesitation in taking his medicines. On the third day for the D.O.T., the client's appointment was due for the Special Health Center and I transported the client there for his early appointment.

Harry was never late for an appointment although he did not have any transportation of his own. He made rapid progress by gaining several pounds within a few weeks. He calls his pills "candies" and he loves taking his medications.

He is one of the most compliant clients I have ever worked with and I sincerely hope that there could be more clients like "Harry". He makes one's job easy and he is also very easy to educate.

His records had been recently transferred to the Special Health Center since all his medical needs will now be taken care of there. He is now also under the supervision of another Health Services Representative which is assigned to that health center. The Health Service Representative for that center told me that she has never worked with a client before that was so cooperative. Clients like "Harry" are seldom seen.

Case XVII: "Annie"

This client was on Preventative Therapy for four months at another health center in the northern region of the county and her records were transferred to this health center when she moved to the Fort Lauderdale area. Bacteriological analysis of her sputum's revealed that the client was positive for Mycobacterium tuberculosis. As a result of this, the client's status was changed from Preventative Therapy to a case.

The client lives in one of those Adult Congregate Homes with a number of other people who are unable to care of themselves. The facility is provided with a staff, which includes about three nurses and some helpers. "Annie" has been attending the health center since April 1993 on a regular basis. Sometimes I transported her to the clinic and back, but since the advent of the D.O.T., I found it necessary to provide her bus tokens for the clinic attendance. The client keeps her clinic appointments and appears to be cooperative. Recently, however, reports from the Bacteriological Laboratory revealed positive sputum.

This has created some major concern and the M.D. has ordered that the client be placed on Directly Observed Therapy as of February 4, 1994. This information was relayed to the client and the nurses in charge of the A.L.C.H. Streptomycin was included in the medication regime for three times weekly. The Tuberculosis Monitor and myself visited the Assisted Living Community Home to find out if one of the nurses there could administer the streptomycin, so as to avoid the client making three visits to the clinic per week. The nurses agreed to give the client the injections three times per week.

In the meantime, I visited the Assisted Living Community Home for the D.O.T. On my first visit for the Directly Observed Therapy, both the client and the nurse's helper asked why I had to come there to see her take her medications since the medications were counted and given to the clients daily as prescribed. I had to go over the whole process again of explaining the D.O.T. and the reason for it although this was discussed previously.

The time arranged for D.O.T. daily was 8:30 AM. I noticed that the clients did not have access to the medications there. The medications are kept in safes and are taken out by one of the nurses and distributed to the clients when required.   There are a number of clients there that are on different types of medications. Whenever I arrived, the nurse in charge of the medications would fetch the medications for "Annie" from the safe and count the amount and deliver them to the client with some juice. This nurse that was in charge of the medications worked from Monday to Friday and she was off duty on Saturday and Sundays.

The first week I visited the A.L.C.H., things looked pretty under control and it appeared as if there was no need for D.O.T. there, but on the following Monday the nurse that was in charge of the medications had an emergency at home, and someone else was administering the medications to the patients. When I arrived for the D.O.T., this person seemed to be unaware of the situation so I explained to her that I was there to see Annie take her medications. She told me to wait for a while because it was breakfast time. I told her I could have the client take the medications if I could just get them, and I would not take up her time. She directed me to the office to check the safe for the medications but I could not find them. Eventually, one of the nurses that were engaged in some other activity came over and got the medications. She apologized for the inconvenience and told me that the lady that I spoke to was just a nurse's aid who was filling in for the nurse in charge of medications.

The client who was on two different types of medications told me that on the Saturday and Sunday the nurse in charge of the medications was off. She was only given one of the medications because the person who was filling in for her could not find one of the medications.

Another observation that I made is that after the medications are delivered to the patients, this nurse who is so busy distributing medications to so many clients, cannot keep her eyes on all the clients taking their medications at the same time. Clients that don't really want to take their medications can just hold them under their tongues and then spit them out later.

The streptomycin that should be administered to the client had to be ordered from Tallahassee and it took about two weeks before the streptomycin arrived. During this period, every time I arrived at the A.L.C.H., the clients would ask me if the streptomycin arrived yet or when it was arriving. I kept answering her questions until finally the streptomycin arrived. They are stored at the health center and distributed to the A.L.C.H.in small quantities each time, which will last about two weeks. After the supply is completed a new supply is refurnished. The days the streptomycin is administered are recorded in a log at the

A.L.C.H. and I keep updating the D.O.T. log of each administration of the streptomycin.

Due to the recent news of the positive sputum of the client from the Bacteriological Lab, the Tuberculosis monitor arranged for a partial PPD testing of the clients who were very close friends to "Annie". The PPD testing was done at the A.L.C.H., and on the day the results of the tests were read, three of the clients' results were positive. This calls for further testing which will be done at a later date. Meanwhile, the client will continue D.O.T. and more sputum specimens will be collected and forwarded to the laboratory for further analysis. The client will also be given an M.D. evaluation within a month at the health center.

Case XVIII: "Jones"

The client was diagnosed for Mycobacterium tuberculosis at the local hospital and is also infected with the HIV virus. On his discharge from the hospital I interviewed the client and completed the Multi-drug Resistant Forms and worksheet for contact investigations. Episodic notes were also completed and submitted with the appropriate forms.

On the day of the interview, the client had a number of different medications, which he brought with him from the hospital. The client was not aware which medication was for tuberculosis and which was for the HIV. I spent some time sorting out these medications and I was instructed to bring in all the old tuberculosis medicines, which would be replaced by a new order.

The client was very cooperative during the interview and assured me that he was willing to attend the health center to receive the services offered. The client was also recommended by the hospital to another health center, which would cater to the client's HIV needs.

The client had been seen by the specialist twice at the health center and has failed to keep the other appointments. He informed me that he was on Medicaid and they would provide transportation to take him to the clinic whenever a ride from his home was not available, but he had to give them advance notice. Despite all these provisions, the client always made some excuse as to why he was unable to attend the health center for his M.D. evaluation. In order for him to continue his therapy his prescriptions are refilled and taken to him whenever his supply of medicines is getting low.

Recently the M.D. ordered that the client be placed on Directly Observed Therapy. I have visited the client and discussed this with him. His D.O.T. order is twice weekly, and we have agreed on the days of Tuesdays and Fridays at 8:00 A.M. Since the D.O.T. has been in force since January 13, 1994, the client has not missed one of his daily appointments. The medication regime consists of three different types of medications and the client is very pleased with this new order. He claims that he is feeling much better since he is not taking too many different medications. The physician at the other health center also reduced his HIV medications to a minimum of one. With the recent changes that seem to have a positive impact on the client, it is hopeful that there will be a change in his behavior in keeping his appointment with the Pulmonary Specialist.

With the increasing number of tuberculosis cases, D.O.T. will continue to be the most important strategy in ensuring that clients are taking their medications. Many institutions have recommended this measure even before the patients are discharged. Physicians at various health centers have also recommended that clients with tuberculosis be placed on Directly Observed Therapy. Every Health Service Representative that is employed by the Broward County health Department had a number of Directly Observed Therapy clients under his or her management.

The various cases, which I have related, do testify to my involvement in Directly Observed Therapy with clients. The cases indicated many successes by enhancing this measure of control, and have also shown a few instances when problems are encountered with clients who do not want to cooperate. D.O.T. programs require a great amount of flexibility on the part of the person managing the client. This is true of persons living at home who are frequently out attending to other things including frequent emergencies. Clients, which are hospitalized, and those living in Adult Living Community Homes and those which are incarcerated, are restricted in their mobility and the frequently adjusting of schedule to accommodate them will not be necessary.

The health department has adopted a new policy recently where all diagnosed cases of Mycobacterium tuberculosis will be placed under Directly Observed Therapy, and measures have also been instituted where court orders will be obtained for the non-compliant cases to be brought to justice which will result in hospitalization at A.G. Holly Hospital in Lantana.

Chapter 17
APPOINTMENT OF SENIOR HUMAN SERVICES PROGRAM SPECIALIST IN TB CONTROL

Shortly after the expansion of our department in the TB Control, we had a new supervisor. He was top executive who was demoted and accepted a position as our supervisor. His title was Senior Human Services Program Specialist (S.H.S.P.S.). He was a very experienced officer in the field of Public Health and took our department to a higher level.

The officer met with me and made enquiry about the nature of my work as a Health Services Representative. He then compiled a special form for the clients, which eliminated a lot of the unnecessary paper work. This form entailed the client's name, address, telephone number, the medication that the client was taking, directions to the client's home, and the name of the H.S.R.

Another change, which was implemented by this supervisor, was the involvement of the H.S.R. in visiting each client on the notification of a doctor or a hospital on a new case of tuberculosis. The H.S.R. would visit the client and give the preliminary training on tuberculosis transmission and prevention, and make an appointment for the client to attend the clinic.

My workload was considerably increased even with the addition of the new staff. I now had a total of sixteen clients on Directly Observed Therapy. The TB monitor at the Sunrise Health Center was amazed at my knowledge in public Health and I was asked by her to visit some of the delinquent cases, which her Public Health nurses had no success with. I visited those clients and discussed tuberculosis transmission and prevention with them and they kept their appointment and attended clinic.

This was a great surprise to the TB monitor and the nurses who had no success in bringing those clients to the clinic. The TB monitor related to my supervisor and the C.H.N.S. of the excellent job that I was performing in that area.

When I applied for the job I had asked the C.H.N.S. about advancement in the field of Public Health and she informed me that within two years if I had excellent work performance I could be promoted to a Case Manager. Well, my appraisals for the job performance were excellent. I had gone over and beyond the call of duty, and I had worked over two years as a Health Services Representative, so I inquired about the upward ascent. The C.H.N.S. informed me that there was no vacancy for a Case Manager at that time but a few weeks after I spoke with the C.H.N.S. I was informed that four of the Public Health Nurses had been promoted to Case Managers. These positions were not even advertised. I had performed the jobs that some of these Public Health nurses had failed to do and despite that, they were promoted to Case Managers.

Well, this was a great disappointment but it was not unusual for me to be treated with impunity. I was also informed that one of the H.S.R. that I had trained was receiving a greater salary than I. I discussed the matter with my Supervisor who told me that there was a similar situation like this among the Pharmacists, which was brought to his attention when he was Administrator and he investigated the matter and had it resolved. He promised to have this matter looked into as early as possible. A meeting was held shortly after and the Nursing Supervisor informed us that the matter was investigated and disparities were revealed among the salaries. She informed us that the matter was referred to the Head Office with recommendations for an adjustment in salaries. The head office rejected the matter on the basis that they would have to upgrade the salaries in other departments which was not possible at this time.

I continued performing my duties and continued to offer the highest standard of service of which I was capable both quantitatively and qualitatively. I understood what facing the challenges of life entailed and did not allow it to break me.

During this period, I was also determined to take my studies to a higher level. There were several courses that were offered by La Salle University in which I was interested. The University was not accredited by the Southern Association of Colleges however. I informed my Supervisor and the C.H.N.S. about the courses and also that the University was not accredited. They considered taking the courses an excellent idea and said that there were many Universities, which were not accredited. I had my transcripts transferred to the University and I proceeded with the course. The courses entailed a lot of reading and writing reports. I had to pay to get my papers typed. I was making good grades and studying a lot of materials on the Administration of Health Services. Some of the concepts that I had grasped, I was also applying in my job.

My major was in Health Administration and I had to submit a topic for my thesis a good while before Graduation. It took me a considerable length of time to come up with a suitable topic. After a few weeks I decided on a topic – "The Role of the Health Services Representatives in the Fight against Tuberculosis." I had a pretty rounded knowledge of the role I was playing in combating tuberculosis but I still had to research the topic more. I submitted my topic to the University and completed the rest of my courses.

I now proceeded to research the subject for my thesis. I spent long hours at the library, gathering information from various books on TB and I planned a few interviews with MD's and Community Health Nursing Supervisor. After I gathered all my materials together with my notes and bibliography, I hired a professional typist to type my material. I had compiled 128 pages of material, which consisted of five chapters. I had not written anything so in depth before. When the typist had completed my book, it was indeed a lovely masterpiece. The cover had the title page and my area of specialization for the PHD in Health

Services Administration. I read through the material and checked for errors, but the typist had done an excellent job. After checking the material, I submitted it to the University. I was also required to submit two recommendations from my Heads of department. One recommendation was derived from my Supervisor and the other from the new C.H.N.S. who was formerly the TB monitor at the Sunrise Health Center. She had succeeded the former C.H.N.S. who had resigned. The recommendations on my behalf were excellent and also stated that with the diverse clientele with which I was involved, they were confident that the courses I had taken would be an asset to the Department.

After completing my courses of studies, my Supervisor had accepted a new position at the hospital in A.G. Holly. A new supervisor came on the scene. He was previously a Health Services Representative who had worked in another area of the Health Field and was now hired to fill in the vacancy. I brought to his attention the stagnation in the Health Services position and he promised to discuss it with the Head of Department. He informed me later on that the Department was considering promoting one of the Health Services Representatives to Senior Health Services Representative. During this period however, a vacancy occurred for a Human Services Program Specialist. There was another applicant from the STD Department who was a Health Services Supervisor in that department and had long years of service beyond mine so he was given the position. All the Health Services Representatives in our department expressed their grouse and that I should have been given the position.

I later received information from La Salle University that I had satisfied all the requirements for my degree in Health Administration. I completed all the graduation requirements and was graduated with a grade point average of 4.0. I informed my Supervisor of my success in completing the course and gave a copy of my Diploma to the Personnel Department and asked that I be reimbursed for my expenditure in taking the courses. They informed me that I should have my Department Head sign a statement requesting my reimbursement. When I informed my Supervisor, he informed me that he would have to contact my previous Supervisor since he was aware of my involvement with the studies and the former C.H.N.S. who was aware of the situation had retired.

He told me that he received a response from the previous Supervisor that he was aware of my studies and that I did it on my own time but he did not believe that the Department would reimburse me for the course taken because the institution was not accredited. I had informed both he and the C.H.N.S. about the courses before I had taken them and they had encouraged me to take the courses and now he did not recommend my reimbursement for the courses.

The challenges of life are varied- disappointment, injustice, hatred, and disparities in salaries, just to name a few: and they are things that we encounter from time to time. The question is "How do you cope with these situations?" There is a poem entitled "If" by Rudyard Kipling, in which Kipling states-

"If you can dream and not make dreams your master,

If you can think and not make thoughts your aim,

If you can meet with trials and disaster, and treat those two imposters just the same;

If you can bear to hear the truth you've spoken twisted by knaves to make a trap for fools, or watch the things you gave your life to broken, and stoop and build 'em up with worn out tools."

Kipling is saying that we should not be overwhelmed by the obstacles that confront us, but we should continue to rise triumphantly above them and continue on the upward path. Despite all the challenges, I was fully persuaded that I was making a contribution in Public Health. The Department was amazed at the number of clients who had fully recovered from tuberculosis and were now making a contribution to society.

Shortly after this, the department hired eight family support workers. These workers required a much lower educational status than Health Services Representatives and they were employed on a temporary basis. The supervisor entrusted all the trainees to me so that I could familiarize them with the necessary forms to be filled for field visits and the proper coding of the forms. After they had mastered these techniques, they were assigned to Health Services Representatives both in the Southern and Northern Health Departments. I was assigned two of these Family support workers for orientation. They were trained for two weeks in the field and then assigned to work in different areas.

After the training of these officers, a position came up for a Health Services Supervisor. I applied for the position and was called for an interview. The interviewers were my supervisor and the C.H.N.S. The interview went very good. I was well prepared and despite the length of the interview there were no questions that baffled me. There was one other person interviewed for the job. He was a Health Services Representative who was hired by my previous Supervisor. The rest of the Health Services Representatives felt that I was most qualified for the position and did not apply for it.

Chapter 18
PROMOTED TO HEALTH SERVICES SUPERVISOR (H.S.S.)

Finally I was officially informed that I was selected for the position. My new title was health Services Supervisor. I was now supervising five Health Services Representatives and eight Family Support Workers. My Supervisor was only supervising three persons, the Human Services Program Manager, a Clerk and Myself. My duties were now different and my responsibilities enlarged. I had acted in a similar position prior to entering the United States and my previous experience was an asset. I had to share an office with another officer and this was an inconvenience. However we tried to accommodate each other as much as possible.

Even after I was promoted to Health Services Supervisor, I had not received an adjustment in my salary. The Supervisor and C.H.N.S. promised to take up this matter with the Personnel Department but I had seen no result so far. Moreover, the Health Services Representative that had competed with me for the H.S.S. position was making a greater salary than I. The Department seemed to have no guideline, which was standardized in starting salary for new employees. After doing some investigation, I discovered that when these new employees were hired they based their salaries according to what they stated that they were earning previously, so that they could maintain a similar lifestyle.

After waiting for a while and there was no adjustment in my salary, I made a visit to the Personnel officer with regards to my salary increase.

The personnel officer assured me that he would research the matter and make the adjustments retroactive from the date of my promotion. Within a week, I received information from the Personnel Department about my salary increase and the effective date. To achieve anything in life, many times we have to take the bull by the horns.

Things were going well during my tenure as H.S.S. I had to fill in a few times for workers who were on leave and a few who encountered problems with clients in the field. As time progressed the H.S.R. that was hired by my previous Supervisor encountered some difficulty with the nurses in the North Regional Health Center. It was alleged that he tried to defame the nurses during their heated argument that they were just RN's and did not possess a college degree as he had. This infuriated the nurses who called the Main Office and made several negative complaints against the officer. This Department was run by nurses and they became very angry with this officer and wanted to have him fired.

This led to an investigation of the officer. There were alleged claims that he was claiming traveling for clients and not seeing them, and that he was not cooperating with the Nurse Case Manager in the area.

Before this, the officer was held in very high regards and had excellent appraisals. On one occasion the officer called in sick, however, he stated that he was feeling much better and called back that he had reported for work. I was asked if I received the message from the officer that he had reported for work. I had not received the message, but the possibility existed that he might have called. There was only one phone in the office, which was shared by the H.S.P.M. and myself. The H.S.P.M. could have deleted the message. During the controversy with the officer, I was recommended for training with the STD department and an investigation of the officer was conducted by my Supervisor. It was a drawn out process and during the investigation the officer was stationed at the Main Office.

After I completed my training at STD, I was asked to cover for the officer in the North Regional Area. This officer was sitting in the office daily doing nothing. The general consensus was that he could not be trusted in the field. After the investigation of the officer was completed a few discrepancies were discovered in his traveling and he was given a few days suspension. After his suspension was completed, he was allowed to resume his normal activities but I had to accompany him in the field for direct supervision. After a few weeks he was returned to his normal activities without accompaniment. He resigned the job about a month later.

After working as a Health Services Supervisor for two years, there was unrest in the Department. There was news that the Department was about to downsize again. Many jobs would be lost and some employees would be demoted. On a list posted was information of the positions that would be eliminated, and the Health Services Supervisor was one of the positions listed. Well, this was the first time that the Department had created this position and just after two years the position was about to be removed. By this time, six of the eight Family Support Workers that were temporarily employed had lost their jobs. Two were made permanent by the Department. I had to give these two further training so that they could take on a little more of the duties of the Health Services Representatives.

Shortly after, I was called to the director of personnel's office. He informed me that the Department had to eliminate my position as H.S.S. but they would keep my name on the list for a while that if a vacancy occurred in another county, I would be recommended for the position. He offered me an alternative, however, that if I remained with the Department and accepted to revert to a H.S.R. position they would pay me my existing salary as H.S.S. After carefully considering the matter, I accepted the latter.

Chapter 19
HEALTH SERVICES SUPERVISOR'S POSITION ELIMINATED

My supervisor would be supervising the staff now. Well, thus ends my job as Health Services Supervisor. By this time, I had become fully aware of the ups and downs in life and I was fully hardened to face the challenges.

My job now as Health Services Representative was nothing new. As a matter of fact, as Health Services Supervisor the pressure was on me in many instances to perform the duties of a Health Services Representative in addition to supervising my staff. I had monthly meetings also and submitted reports to the Supervisor and C.H.N.S. Well, I was now relieved of these additional responsibilities. My chief focus would now be on my clients and training new employees.

It was then discovered that there was a link between TB and HIV. Clients who were immunosuppressed were more likely to contract Mycobacterium Tuberculosis. I was also trained as a HIV counselor and occasionally counseled clients at the clinic. There were few clients, who declined the HIV test, but many were tested, some of which received the sad news that they were HIV positive. The clients that tested positive were placed on several antiviral drugs in addition to the TB drug that they were taking. The Department was also giving nutritional supplements to those clients as well as other food coupons, which were redeemable at Publix and Winn Dixie stores.

There was now an increase in clients and reduction in staff. The department acquired a van and a driver to alleviate the difficulty for clients to reach the clinic for medical evaluation and refilling medications. Many times this driver did not show up on clinic days and Health Services Representatives and the Family Support Workers had to pick up clients for their clinic visits. The Departments had also acquired bus passes, which were utilized by some of the clients for which the bus was easily accessible.

The Department had now taken measures to renovate the main office in which we were located and we had to move to the North Regional Health Center. It took a considerable period of time to pack our records into boxes and then they were labeled for the office, which we were located. It took some time to settle down in our new location. We still had to ply between there and the Main Office as was deemed necessary. At first we were informed that we would be at our new location for about six months but we were there for nearly two years. The renovation seemed to take a much longer time than was anticipated. When it was all completed and we were relocated at our former office, everything was completely changed.

Each officer had what was known as a cubicle equipped with a chair and desk and a computer. The space was definitely designated for a single person. Only Supervisors and Administrators had offices. It was amazing how things had changed in the Department. When I was hired first, I had my own office. All Health Services Representatives had their own office. When I became a Supervisor I had to share an office with someone else, and now both Nurses and Health Services Representatives occupied a space so small, you could barely turn in it. In addition, you could only enter your location by swiping your Identification Card. Every employee was given a new ID.

Your ID was required to be worn at all times for security purposes. If you happened to forget your ID, you would have to keep knocking at the door until someone let you in. Many workers became frustrated with the changes but they were gradually accepted over time.

Chapter 20
RELOCATION OF MY MOTHER TO FLORIDA

After readjustment to our new office, I received a call from my mother in New York that she wanted to come and visit my family. My mother had not seen the children from since she left Jamaica, which was over ten years ago. Her trip was planned for two weeks later and I arranged to pick her up at the airport. We had enough space to accommodate her but my main concern was about the one bathroom that we had. This home had three bedrooms and one bathroom and with someone new in our family, I wondered if there would be any inconvenience on her part. Our family was very easy to adjust to any situation. Previously, my sister-in-law and her family visited us and we encountered no problem. I was a bit concerned about my mother, however, since she had been living alone for sometime without any entanglement.

Well, the day came and I picked up my mother at the airport accompanied by Irvin Jr. She was elated to see us and did not appear anyway exhausted from her trip. On our way home she talked briefly about her trip and enquired how Irvin Jr. was doing in school. We arrived home and my mother was reunited with the family, and shortly afterwards dinner was served. Dinner was greatly enjoyed by everyone and my mother commended my wife for being an excellent cook. We explained the bathroom situation to my mother but surprisingly she did not seem to be bothered by this situation. My mother informed us that she had just retired from her job as a paramedic but she was having some trouble with the new people that moved into the complex in which she was living.

She informed us that the people were of Spanish descent and she, who was a born-again Christian, was having so much strange encounters in her apartment that she believed they were engaged in witchcraft. They wanted her to move out of her apartment so that they could have it for their family.

My mother stayed for two weeks and returned to New York. One month after she returned, she informed me that the disturbances with these people had worsened and she reluctantly had decided to give up her apartment. She had been living there for over ten years and it was like her own home. She had no relatives in New York, and she did not like Florida because she said it was too hot down here. However, I encouraged her to move to Florida, so that she could be near her relatives. She finally decided and relocated to Florida. She stayed with us for one year and decided that she would add a room and a bathroom to our home since she did not have enough money to purchase a home of her own. I started to check out the information for the renovation and discovered that I would be required to resurvey my property since the previous survey was too old.

I contacted the surveyor about this and a date was finalized for the survey to be done. During this interval, I met a Real Estate Broker and our discussion lead to my mother's situation. I had told my mother previously that she would not be able to qualify for a home since she was not gainfully employed. However, this Broker told me that he would be able to get her qualified for a townhouse or condo. I informed my mother about this new information and canceled the surveyor's appointment.

Within seven weeks the Broker got my mother qualified for a two bedroom, one bath condo and she was relocated to her own place. She would be staying just three miles away so that we could see her quite frequently. I visited my mother on my time off from work, and took her to the grocery store and church when she needed a ride. She was an ardent student of the bible and we frequently had Bible discussions and I was amazed at her knowledge of the Scriptures. Sometimes we differed on certain points because I had now become an Adventist and worshipped on the Sabbath while she worshipped on Sundays. There were certain truths, which we agreed on however.

My mother appeared in good health. She exercised frequently and did volunteer work in the community. She baked the best corn bread and potato puddings, and was an expert in embroidery work. Occasionally, she would also prepare a meal for us and bring it over. This was enjoyed by everyone. She was the only person that had gone to the trouble to prepare a meal for my family. My wife was the one that was always preparing meals for others on holidays and other special occasions.

As time progressed, my mother sold her condo and bought a lovelier one consisting of two bedroom, two bathrooms, living room, etc. She was also living closer to us, and within closer range of the hospital and shopping centers. Shortly after, I had also moved to a location, which was just two miles within range of her home. We saw each other frequently and I assisted her on errands that were out of her reach.

In course of time, however, she bought a used car and was able to transport herself around. I had some new tires installed on the car since the other ones were showing signs of being thread worn. She enjoyed the comfort of her car for a good while and then she began to experience some mechanical difficulties. I took the car to my mechanic and had the problem corrected and covered the bill for her.

As time went by more problems emerged and she figured that the car was costing too much for repairs and decided to sell it. Well, this was not a problem; I would still be available to take her around whenever it was necessary to do so.

Prior to the Graduation of one of our boys from F.A.U., my mother complained that she was not feeling so well. She had not been ill since arriving in Florida except for a bout with the flu, which was shaken off in a few days. She attended the Graduation but she said that her appetite was not so good. She had frequent check-ups at the doctor prior to this and everything was normal. At work, whenever I was asked about my mother I always responded that she was in perfect health. On this trip to the doctor, the doctor informed her that her blood work was not looking very good and ordered further tests. She was also referred to a specialist.

Later on I discovered that my mother was having some problem in swallowing. I brought her some of her favorite fruits such as mangoes and peaches. She was not enjoying her favorite fruits as she used to. She had extreme difficulties with her peaches. Further on, she was having difficulty swallowing even yogurt.

The specialist had recommended that a feeding tube should be installed in the abdominal region and admitted her to the hospital for the procedure. She agreed to the procedure and the operation was successfully performed. After this, my mother could only be fed with a nutritious liquid protein substance through the tube. I thought that this would only be a temporary situation but it lasted for a while and so I had my mother's medical records transferred to my physician after a discussion with her.

The doctor gave her a thorough physical examination and recommended her to see a specialist for her throat condition. The specialist examined her and tried to do a biopsy but the material that she obtained for the biopsy was small and she explained that she needed a larger specimen but she would send it anyway for examination. I could see that it was very painful to obtain the specimen for the biopsy. The specialist suspected cancer. However, the specimen was too small to confirm the disease. She recommended surgery, however, and set a date for her admission to the hospital.

My mother asked her several questions about the surgery and her answer to some of the questions were uncertain. My mother who had worked in the hospital for years as a paramedic was fully aware of what this type of surgery entails. On the morning of her admission to the hospital, she decided not to take the surgery. Other specialists were consulted and recommendations were made for chemotherapy. By then my mother began coughing up blood. I took her to the chemotherapy in the evenings. The chemotherapy took such a toll on her that I had to actually lift her up to put in the car. I could not believe that her strength had declined so rapidly. I spent long hours with her at nights accompanied by my wife. She usually told us to go home because it was too late. She was accustomed to sleep in the dark and many times when she asked us to put out the light in her room, we still stayed around when she thought we were gone.

Recommendations were made by the doctor for some Nursing Personnel to come in at intervals to assist my mother with feeding and other duties. Prior to this, I had to assist her with the feeding because I observed that she had difficulty in dispensing nutritional supplements in the tube. An oxygen cylinder was also provided to assist her with breathing.

All her grandchildren dropped in frequently and rendered whatever aid they could provide for their grandmother especially her granddaughter since she could be of greater assistance in many ways. I would visit her in the early mornings before I went to work and would drop in during lunch hours. There was a nurse who was a good friend of the family who was working at the hospital just across the street from where my mother was living. She would visit my mother every time she was on break and made sure that she was okay. Many times when I dropped in to see my mother during lunch breaks she was there. I expressed how much I appreciated her thoughtfulness.

Sometimes on weekends my wife and I would just walk it over as part of our exercise routine early in the morning. On this Sunday morning, we walked it over and observed my mother was still sleeping. We had left 12:20 AM in the night so we did not disturb her. She said that she generally got the best sleep in the mornings. We sang hymns and read Scriptures before we left the night. She was always talking about the Lord and she enjoyed these beautiful hymns and Scripture passages. On one occasion, she seemed to be whispering something and when we asked her what was happening she responded that she was saying her prayers.

Chapter 21

THE DEATH AND BURIAL OF MY MOTHER

After breakfast that Sunday morning, I went back to see my mother and discovered that she was still in the position that I had left her previously. I called her and discovered that she was awake and she was trying to talk but just couldn't utter the words for me to understand. I called my wife and the children who came speedily. My mother was making some gruesome sounds. The Emergency Crew was called in and I accompanied them to the hospital. The nurse asked us to remain outside for a while until they attended to her. We were shortly called in. By that time, she was no longer making those gruesome sounds. We tried to speak comforting words to her but there was no response.

I couldn't believe that she was dying. Although she was ill for sometime the thought of her final departure was horrifying. As we lingered around her bed she appeared so peaceful and radiance encompassed her. Finally, there was a deep gasp a quick shiver and my mother departed from this life.

The Psalmist says, *"The days of our years are threescore years and ten; and if by reason of strength they be fourscore years, yet is there strength labor and sorrow; for it is soon cut off and we fly away." Psalm 90:10.* My mother had reached her eighty-third birthday. I thought she would be around for a longer time. She ate right, she exercised, and she drank distilled water that I supplied her with regularly. Many people that were not observing the laws of health outlived her by a number of years. Well, Job says, *"the Lord gave, and the Lord hath taken away; blessed be the name of the Lord." Job 1:21.*

This was the first time that I observed a member of my family passed away. I was not present when my grandfather and my grandmother departed this life.

Well, it became time to prepare for my mother's burial. The department with which I was employed gave employees two days off for deaths of their near relatives. I requested a few days additional to make arrangements for the funeral. I was the only child for my mother and it was my responsibility to have things arranged. My mother bought a burial plot in New York but when she relocated to Florida, she did not sell the plot, but purchased one of those Pre-Med Funeral Plans. She looked at some memorial parks in Florida and there was one memorial park that she liked for her final resting place, which was Lauderdale Memorial Park.

My mother had even picked out the casket that she liked. The day that I took her to the funeral home to choose the casket I stayed away from getting involved in her choice. My mother used to frequently talk about death, and did not seem to be scared of death at all. I always asked her why she talked about death so much, and she would respond that when you reached a certain age you had to expect death.

The Director of the funeral home advised me that if I chose one of the other two memorial parks for the burial instead of the Lauderdale Memorial Park, the price for the burial plot would be considerably lower. However, I decided on the one that my mother liked. I believe that someone's wish should still be respected even in his or her death. The funeral Director took me to the plot and I paid several hundred dollars more for the burial plot and had everything settled.

The minister of her church was contacted personally and arrangements were made for the date and time of the funeral. Relatives and friends both at home and abroad were notified of her final farewell. The Director and his staff at the funeral home were most courteous and helpful during our time of need. Flowers and cards expressing sympathy came from friends and co-workers near and far.

My wife and daughter assisted me in planning the program. I had not been involved in these types of proceedings before. I perused through some of my mother's belongings. She had acquired some certificates, which I was not even aware of. I was astonished to discover that my mother was an ordained minister. I had been aware of her Scriptural in-depth but unaware of her qualifications. During the planning of the program, members of the family and friends expressed what part they would like to play in the ceremony. My mother had two sisters in Jamaica who explained that because of ill health they would not be able to attend the funeral, but selected the Scripture passages that they would like to be read.

After the program was drawn up, I was visited by my wife's brother-in-law and he gave me some insights of a few additional things that I could include in the eulogy. The delivery of the eulogy had fallen on me.

Having completed all preparations for the funeral, the final day came for the Home-Coming of Ursula Cecile Benjamin (the late). We were picked up at the Home by the funeral Director who offered a prayer and escorted us to the church, the Hearse traveling ahead of us. Folks were gathered at the Chapel attired in their mournful arrays. I paid the last respects to my mother lying helplessly in that casket. The pastor commenced the ceremony with prayer. The organist tuned to the jubilant voices echoing Amazing Grace. My wife bellowed a solo. *"Oh what a sunrise with angelic voice."* There were moments of expressions by folks paying tributes to my late mother.

Her grandson Dwight contributed a lovely poem that he had written entitled "My Beautiful Dream." He was given a tremendous applause and folks solicited copies of the same.

Then it was time for the eulogy. I approached the platform gracefully and eulogized my late mother in terms that she would be proud of if she could hear me. I left no ground uncovered. At the end of my deliberation the crowd was moved with such adoration that it took some time for them to be settled.

The minister then delivered his brief sermon and the ceremony concluded with the singing of the hymn *"It is well with my soul."* We then traveled to Lauderdale Memorial Park for the interim.

At the graveside the committal of the body was done by the minister. Hymns were sung, and the final benediction was given. As I departed from my mother's graveside I was greatly saddened by the death of my mother. Many persons make an outward burst of tears and relieve their tension but I kept it all inside and underwent the pain for a very long time. How short and unreal life is. My mother who was born on the 8th of January 1920 departed this life on the 8th of June 2003. Those 83 years seemed to evaporate so rapidly. Life offers so much sadness and grief yet it is loved and adored by everyone.

On arrival home, the mourners who stopped by were refreshed before returning to their respective abodes.

Chapter 22

PLANNING FOR RETIREMENT

With the funeral procession for my mother now passed, it was time to divert my attention to other matters of interest. The department offered a Deferred Compensation Plan and the Deferred Retirement Option Plan.

The Deferred Retirement Option Plan, commonly known as DROP, is a plan that employees can enter at the age of 60 years old. The plan lasted for five years and your DROP benefit is based on the option selected at retirement, and will accrue with interest and cost of living adjustments for the duration of DROP participation. Upon termination of DROP, you have 60 days to elect one of the following methods of payment for the DROP benefits.

1. Lump Sum: All accrued benefits plus interest; less tax shall be paid to the DROP participant or the surviving beneficiary.

2. Direct Rollover: All accrued DROP benefits plus interest shall be paid from the DROP directly to the custodian of the eligible retirement plan.

3. Partial Lump Sum: A portion of the accrued DROP benefits shall be paid to the DROP participant or surviving spouse, less IRS tax, and

the remaining DROP benefits shall be transferred directly to the custodian of an eligible retirement plan.

If you did not make an election of one of the above methods of payment within the 60-day period, the Division of retirement would pay to you the accrued benefits in a lump sum less tax. If you failed to terminate on your DROP termination date, your retirement will be null and void, and your membership established retroactively to the date the DROP started.

I was enrolled in the Deferred Retirement Option Plan for four years. I should have enrolled in the plan for a year earlier to complete the five years that the plan offered, but due to lack of information I lost one year from the plan. The plan provided employees with printouts of the amount that they would accumulate in the plan during the period that they were enrolled in it and also the beginning and ending dates.

At the termination of my DROP I rolled over the amount I had accumulated to the Deferred Compensation Plan. The tax can be avoided for a while if the funds are rolled over into an eligible plan, but eventually you will have to pay the tax on accessing the funds. The tax rate was twenty percent and that was a very big chunk of your savings. In my opinion it is better to pay tax as you earn.

Well, having completed my DROP period I asked the Division of Retirement if it was possible to complete the additional year in DROP since I entered the Deferred Retirement Option Plan one year later than I should have but I was told that it would only be possible if I was in instructional. I terminated my DROP on the 21st of January in 2006, accessed my accumulated savings and paid the required IRS tax. I spent fifteen years with the Department of Health. It had been filled with ups and downs but I was convinced that I had made some contribution for the betterment of health in the lives of clients, and I have impacted the lives of many co-workers positively in training and other areas.

If I had been giving the opportunity to enter the Department of Health earlier I would have had a greater influence on the Department. One of the shortcomings of the Department was their inability to recognize and respect people that have great knowledge and experience if they do not possess a four-year college degree, and this was particularly true of the Broward County Health Department. The DADE County Health Department for example, has taken a different stand in this matter.

Chapter 23
RELOCATING TO MY HOMELAND

Having now retired from my job in the department of Health, it was now time to relocate in the country of my birth. My wife and I had made several trips to Jamaica during our vacation times and have kept abreast of the many changes that have taken place during our migration to the United States.

During our visit we had looked on several small cottages, but the price for them was far beyond our reach. Even lots for sale carried high price as well. Our accumulated savings, plus social security and retirement benefits placed us in a very low financial standing. In the earlier months of 2008 we visited Jamaica and looked around at a few places and found nothing that was in our reach for purchase. So we returned to the States and decided that we might have to reside there for a longer time than was anticipated.

On our return to the United States I bought a Camry owing to the fact I had given my 1995 Ford Escort to one of our sons. Shortly after purchasing the car, I had a call from my friend who had been looking around to see if he could find anything that we could afford. He saw a little cottage two bedrooms and one bath with a little studio advertised for sale. I told him to contact the owner for the price seemed to be one that we could meet although it could be quite a stretch. The owner of the premises was contacted and a date was set for us to view the premises and meet the owner.

On the date appointed our friend took us to meet the owner of the property. On our arrival the owner had arrived ahead of time and allowed us to view the property. I liked it despite the repairs, which I saw that it needed. There were fruit trees such as breadfruit, mangoes, pears, june plums, pomegranate, bananas, and ackee etc. In addition, there was an excellent view of the ocean from the cottage.

We decided on the price factor and set a date to make a deposit and bind the agreement. My friend took us to Mandeville on the appointed date to the Attorney's Office to have the agreement drawn up. We decided to utilize the services of the seller's Attorney in order to curtail the cost. The transaction went smoothly and my friend was empowered to do the closing cost, since I had to return to the States to tie up some loose ends. In about a month and a few weeks after my return I received information that the title transfer was completed and my friend had closed the deal.

The final preparations were made for our return to the island. My wife did all the packing of the essential items that we wanted to accompany us. I wanted to take my Camry but when I checked the duty that I had to pay, I just could not afford it, and had to sell it taking a loss. We arrived in Jamaica on the 30th July 2008 at 8:00 A.M. We got our entire luggage with the exception of a few barrels, which we had to pick up at Montego Bay at a later date.

After spending a few days in Fort George we decided to go and take position of our small cottage. Our friend was anxiously awaiting us to hand over the keys and the documents. He also informed us that a few days earlier when he visited the cottage he observed that the studio was over flooded. A leak was discovered in the lavatory. He did some temporary repairs to avert the leak, but I discovered that this needed a plumber to do a complete check and affect the repairs.

We bought some cleaning agents and spent the entire day cleaning the apartment, but it was evident that a lot more cleaning was needed. Arrangement was made for further cleaning with a helper to assist us. After a few days we collected the rest of our stuff at Montego Bay and completed the cleaning process and were ready to move in.

On the day of our transition the small truck that was transporting us encountered some mechanical problem just about two miles away from our destination. This would take a couple of hours to get a mechanic and affect the repairs, so we took a taxi home and awaited the arrival of our belongings.

It was not long after our arrival that we received a call from the owner of the vehicle that the repairs were completed and he was on his way. In about ten minutes he arrived and delivered all our belongings.

Our daughter and her husband who was visiting in the island stopped by and spent two days with us at our new abode. Their baby Michaela also accompanied them. They were delighted to be able to spend some time at the Beach before their departure.

Well here we are in Priory getting adjusted to our original Jamaican lifestyle. We have a lovely view of the beach from our cottage and to access the beach we just have to get across the other side of the street. Everything seems to come with a price however; Mr. K.O. Morris our friend informed us from the first contact that he had some concern about the noise. It did not take us long to acknowledge that fact. The Parish Council of St. Ann has leased the beach to a private party and they have kept dances on Wednesdays and Sunday nights with extremely loud music. The residents around this area have become immune to this type of lifestyle.

There are other minor problems, which we have encountered but this will be subsided as soon as we make our fence more secured. I was also alarmed by an overwhelming water bill in the amount of Forty One Thousand Three Hundred and Seventy Three Dollars and Thirty-Four Cents. I figured that this was an error on the part of the utilities company and asked to have the matter investigated. After the investigation was completed, it was alleged that this was due to a leaking water closet and I had to pay the entire excessive bill.

Having put most of the disturbing things into proper place I decided to make a small addition to our cottage, which entailed a room and a bathroom. An architect was contacted for an estimate and within a short time the construction was underway.

I could not believe the gust of dust that was created and the sound of unending noise.

Oh the measuring and lining and marking

And fastening and lengthening and strengthening

And digging and plugging and logging

Deciding, confiding, abiding

And loading and bonding and binding

Deceiving, conceiving and receiving.

Excavating, cementing and casting, and blasting

And bickering and sandering and plastering and rendering

And drying and dying and lying and plying.

Unfolding and holding, embolding and scolding

And washing and bashing and lashing and squashing.

And hinting and linting and pointing and painting

And sprouting and shouting, and outing and routing.

And blocking and knocking and flocking and locking.

And hammering and tammering and clammering and jammering.

And bouncing and pouncing and racing and placing.

Oh the pounding and founding and abounding and grounding.

And so to the ending, so glamorously bending

The noisome sounds at last are receding.

Aghast, and Alas, there is silence at last.

And now that it's over, what a blessed relief.

My deafening ears are gladly relieved.

My compassionate wife who had voluntarily prepared lunch for the crew, on several occasions can now utilize her time in other activities. Our studio, which was temporarily used as storage for the materials, and changing room for the crew, is now completely renovated and is also rented to a lady temporarily.

The new addition of a room and bathroom to our home has now been completed and furnished and has become the master bedroom. The panoramic view of the ocean is fantastic as we observe the ships passing by. The dances at the beach continue mostly on Sundays and Wednesdays. This annoyance has brought some concern about relocating to a more peaceful neighborhood. We have acquired another lot of land in an area, which is quieter but lacks the panoramic view.

We listed our home for sale for a short time. There were a few interested parties but they seemed to miss the mark for qualification financially. After re-evaluating the situation, we decided to withdraw the sale. The noise still exists but it subsided greatly. We are now in the process of improving the lot, which we purchased with the intention of offering it for sale.

In the meantime I am busy in improving our property with a vegetable garden, which consists of calaloo, peas, beans, corns, spinach, peppers, sweet potatoes, tomatoes, and a lot of plants for herbal teas. I have also planted additional fruit trees such as Jamaican apples, plums, pomegranates, noni etc. Banana and plantains are also part of the food group. My love for gardening is also strong and I am a fervent believer that we should produce most of what we eat.

The challenges of life are varied and complex and present themselves as hurdles we must face continually. They will place enormous strain on our strength and vitality but by perseverance, and tolerance, we can defeat our foes and triumph victoriously to win the prize.

ACKNOWLEDGEMENTS

I would like to express my thankfulness for quotes utilized from the following authors:

A) The authorized King James Version of the Holy Bible
   1) Psalm 90:10
   2) Job 1:20
   3) "If" by Rudyard Kipling"